Praise for
Your Diet is Driving Me Crazy

"Finally, a book that encourages couples to understand the vital role food plays in their relationship. Share it with a loved one over a candlelit dinner and start on the road to happier, healthier eating together."

—LUCY DANZIGER,
editor-in-chief of *Self* magazine

Your Diet is
Driving Me Crazy

About the Authors

© Beverly Brosius

Cynthia Sass, MPH, MA, RD, is a registered dietitian and nationally recognized health and nutrition expert who has been working with couples on their food issues for ten years. She is a national media spokesperson for the American Dietetic Association, the largest group of food and nutrition professionals in the country, and she teaches at the University of South Florida. She is seen regularly by forty thousand Tampa Bay residents who watch her *Life Matters* health segments on the local CBS affiliate's morning show. She has been quoted in *The New York Times, The Wall Street Journal,* the *Chicago Tribune, Glamour, Seventeen, Cosmopolitan, Woman's Day, Ladies Home Journal,* and many other publications. She lives in Tampa, Florida.

© Jonathan B. Ragle

Denise Maher is a freelance writer whose stories about health, fitness, nutrition, and relationships have appeared in *Self, Cosmopolitan, Details, Time Out New York, Mademoiselle, New York,* and many other publications. She lives in Brooklyn, New York.

CYNTHIA SASS, MPH, MA, RD, AND
DENISE MAHER

Your Diet is Driving Me Crazy

WHEN FOOD CONFLICTS

GET IN THE WAY OF

YOUR LOVE LIFE

To Sandy,
Denise Maher

Marlowe & Company
New York

YOUR DIET IS DRIVING ME CRAZY:
When Food Conflicts Get in the Way of Your Love Life
Copyright © 2004 by Cynthia Sass and Denise Maher

Published by
Marlowe & Company
An Imprint of Avalon Publishing Group Incorporated
245 West 17th Street • 11th Floor
New York, NY 10011-5300

Library of Congress Cataloging-in-Publication Data is available.
ISBN 1-56924-474-X

9 8 7 6 5 4 3 2 1

Designed by Pauline Neuwirth, Neuwirth & Associates, Inc.

Printed in the United States of America
Distributed by Publishers Group West

I dedicate this to my husband Jack Bremen for his never-ending love, support, patience, compromise, and humor, and for allowing me to share our real-life stories in this book.

And to my beautiful sister, Diane Salvagno, for her unconditional love, friendship, honesty, and laughter.
—CS

For Mike.
—DM

Contents

Introduction

This book is about how your relationship with food inter-
sects with your relationship with your partner. If you learn to
understand your own relationship with food, you can help your
partner understand his or hers, enrich your romantic relationship, and improve your physical health. In essence, it's about
how to cope with problematic food issues so you can relate to
each other better. It's about eating in sync with each other, with
your body's needs, and with the world around you.

Either partner's food issues can interfere with eating and intimacy. Food issues are anything with the potential to become a
small or severe conflict between two people. These issues stem
from food personalities (what one likes to eat) as well as food
relationships (the role food plays in one's life). Your food personality is what you like and dislike and that's pretty static. Your food
relationship is the role food plays in your life, and that changes
all the time.

Let's say your grandma fed you tomato soup and grilled cheese
sandwiches when you were young. Most likely, that familiar

favorite has become a healthy part of your food personality. But if you've come to rely on three or four sandwiches to deal with financial stress, it's taken on an unhealthy role in your life. Your dysfunctional relationship with food may cause problems in your overall life and your romantic relationship because you're using food as a coping mechanism instead of finding a healthy way to deal.

The most troublesome food conflicts come from one partner's complicated relationship with food: he or she goes on a diet, eats for emotional reasons or struggles with body image. On the other side of the spectrum, couples' more straight forward food issues come from differences in tastes and food personalities: one is a picky eater while the other is adventurous, one is a vegetarian and the other is a carnivore.

If you've picked up this book you're attuned to the idea that your food issues might be adversely affecting your romantic relationship. Now you can begin to explore the issues that hold you back from a better relationship and better health. In addition to interfering with intimacy, food issues are obstacles to weight loss, cholesterol control, stable blood pressure, and increased energy levels. They're the reasons many of us fail to find health and weight loss success. Until you learn how to really resolve them, as I'll explain in this book, they're bound to haunt you.

Take a look at the table of contents. Several of the seventeen chapters should apply to you and yours. Does one person police what the other eats? Do you both struggle to find time to eat better? Does food or hunger influence your mood? Is one of you on a diet? Do either of you use food as a coping mechanism? We all deal with these types of food conflicts. They're common, but not necessary. We can get past them.

Partners are in a unique position to help us improve our relationships with food. They know us better than anyone else. They share our meals and observe our daily food habits. They love and trust us. They can confront us, be honest with us, and listen to us better than anyone else.

Partners also have the most to gain. If you're turning to grilled cheese instead of your mate, the feelings the food is suppressing will surface elsewhere in your relationship. If you use food as a coping mechanism, as so many of us do, you're probably disconnected from your feelings, which makes it harder for you to talk about them. In a way, you're cheating on your partner with food.

Partners with strong food personalities can contribute to plain old compatibility conflicts. A pair may have opposing philosophies about the use of mustard or pepper or drive each other crazy with annoying eating habits like talking with a mouth full of food. One might fail to grasp the importance of diet Coke or Reese's Peanut Butter Cups in the other's life. Partners may be part of the food problem, but more importantly, they are part of the solution!

Innocently or deliberately, they can hinder our healthy eating attempts. But they can also—and here's what's crucial—help those efforts. As much as they can get in the way of our health goals, they can clear the way for them. And they don't even have to change their diets; they just need to let us change ours. The hidden reason you haven't lost weight or lowered your cholesterol may be that you underestimate the importance of your partner's help or don't know how to ask him or her for support.

When I met my husband Jack, our food personalities and eating habits couldn't have been further apart. I was vegetarian, he was a carnivore. He was raised in the South, I grew up in the North. He loved spicy foods while I couldn't handle the mildest jalapeño. I religiously ate every three or four hours, while he often skipped meals. I always had high fiber cereal for breakfast, but he only ate big country breakfasts on weekends. I was a diet Coke girl, he lived for Dr Pepper. He loved beer, I was a wine drinker. Despite our food differences, we fell in love, and had to find ways to eat together. In the beginning it was cute. Halfway through my veggie burger, I'd watch in amazement while the "condiment king" (as his friends called him) garnished his chicken sandwich with black pepper, salt, hot peppers, mustard, and Tabasco Sauce. But that was only adorable for so long.

Eventually our food conflicts became irritating. I'd want pasta and he'd want Mexican. I'd be ready for lunch and he'd still be stuffed from his Saturday morning Grand Slam special. While some of my healthy habits have rubbed off on him over the years (he's lost fifty pounds since we've met), our fundamental food personalities still differ. But we've found ways to compromise. I'll explain how throughout the book.

I've counseled thousands of people over ten years and studied health sciences extensively to understand how people can change. After I earned my master's degree in nutrition with a concentration in community counseling—which means I studied counseling and psychology—I felt I was still missing the key to change. As I counseled more and more people, the role that relationships, families, and culture played in my clients' lives became more and more apparent. I'd have an exciting, promising session with a motivated client, but once that person returned to an unsupportive partner or family, he or she resumed the same unhealthy lifestyle or diet. To be better prepared to offer counseling in such situations, I went back to school again, this time to get another master's degree in community and family health education. This taught me to understand the roles social relationships play in individual health-related behaviors. To put it plainly, I learned to understand how a person's partner or family influences how healthfully he or she lives. Because food is such a fundamental part of our personal and social lives, nutrition cannot be discussed in isolation. My training lets me look at the big picture and examine a person's diet in the context of his or her life. It's enabled me to help thousands of clients learn more about themselves, their relationships, and how to make long-term successful lifestyle changes.

Many couples I've counseled come to realize their own food conflicts with a little self-exploration. Some eventually see that they've struggled with subtle eating tensions for a long time without seeing the actual problem. Other times, one partner clearly sees a food conflict the other partner can't. Some couples

immediately recognize that one or both of them have an inten-
sively personal relationship with food that fuels arguments, but
have become so accustomed to problems that they don't think
they're solvable.

Until you read this, you may not realize that your partner may
encourage you to overeat, postpone meals, or eat when you don't
really want to. You may have suspected but not confirmed that
your partner sabotages your diet. Or you may know that at times
you're a food cop, telling him or her what not to eat, but not
understanding there are more effective ways to encourage
healthy eating that won't irritate your partner.

Your Diet Is Driving Me Crazy offers questionnaires, case
studies, and exercises to help you recognize the common food-
related issues many of us consciously and unconsciously struggle
with. It will help you see what those issues are, how they affect
your relationship and your health and how to solve them. I call
this three-step process food therapy: exploring, identifying, and
solving food issues. After exploring and identifying your food conflicts, you will learn how to explain eating problems to your
partner, ask for help overcoming them, and execute the solution
prescribed. I developed my SANITY model to make this process
simple. SANITY stands for the key food therapy concepts:

See the problem.
Ask your partner to understand the problem and support you.
Negotiate a compromise.
Imagine creative solutions.
Take advantage of outside resources.
Yuck it up and use humor to dissolve tension.

Every food conflict can be resolved using one or more SANITY
letter or concept. These stimulating ideas will help you draw out
the best solutions to your particular problem from inside yourself. I'll explain each letter as it applies to the sample food fights
that fill this book.

Finally, just a couple of other things to say at the outset. One: It's not as hard as it sounds. And two: You don't need to change who you are, what you like to eat, or how you live your life. But you will need to explore your food issues, delve into the food conflicts they cause, and take steps to overcome them. In short, you'll have to get to know each other better to find out how food is bringing you together and pushing you apart. Whether you've just met or have been married for forty years, there's something here to help couples discover a solution to nearly every imaginable food conflict situation. Let's get started on making the first move toward making those discoveries.

1

You Left the Milk Out Again!

DEALING WITH YOUR PARTNER'S
IRRITATING FOOD HABITS

I hear about a lot of minor food issues that irritate my clients. They might complain about a partner who doesn't do the dishes, leaving no available cereals bowls in the morning, or, he/she forgets to put the milk back in the fridge or constantly leaves toast crumbs in the butter. The list of ways partners' food habits can annoy us is endless!

When your partner puts the empty orange juice carton back in the fridge or eats standing in the kitchen instead of sitting at the table, it can rub you the wrong way. However, these food-related annoyances aren't really about food itself. While they may get on your last nerve, they probably aren't affecting your health or seriously rocking your relationship. Food nuisances may be simple bad habits that have become bothersome. They also might be symptoms of other relationship problems, such as a lack of communication, lack of consideration, or even unequal separation of household duties. These kinds of irritations play out in other non-food ways as well. For example, the partner who leaves crumbs in the butter may also neglect to wipe his shoes before tracking mud on the tile. The one who puts the empty carton back in the fridge may also fail to replace an empty toilet paper roll. It's important to recognize the difference between simple food *nuisances* and true food *conflicts*. Fortunately, food nuisances—relationship or communication issues that just happen to play out through food—are fairly easy to resolve. Doing so can have a positive impact on other trying behaviors your partner repeats. True food conflicts, on the other hand, take a bit more work and have deeper consequences. Food conflicts are fundamentally about food and can cause serious detriment to the health of one or more people as well as the health of the relationship.

This book is dedicated to solving the major food conflicts that interfere with intimacy, such as when one partner militantly polices what the other eats, sabotages the other's healthy diet, or excessively expresses love with food. However, addressing the minor problems is a great way to start thinking and talking about the role of food in your relationship, too. Exploring pet peeves allows you and your partner to start a dialogue with one another and delve into the major food conflicts. Many times, it's easier to start small. Petty food issues can be resolved with honesty, my first principle of food therapy, and good communication. Let's look at the first step in the SANITY model. **s**, seeing the problem honestly, is the most important idea for solving petty food issues. Being honest is the first step toward a healthy discourse and will help you acknowledge your true feelings, uncover a problem, explain it to your partner, and start working toward a solution. Honesty makes it possible for you to finally lay all your cards on the table. Talking to your partner—and I mean really talking ("You left the milk out again!" doesn't count)—can solve the problem and pave the way for bigger, more difficult changes.

FOOD PET PEEVES

Take a look at the list of some common, but nowhere near all-inclusive list of food pet peeves. Do any of them sound familiar?

- Eating with the television on
- Putting an empty container back into the refrigerator
- Loudly slurping soup, cereal, or coffee
- Talking with food in his or her mouth
- Leaving all the food shopping or preparation to the other person
- Failing to buy the other's favorite foods or brands
- Keeping a disorganized refrigerator or leaving old food for the other to throw out
- Being noncommittal about what to have for dinner
- Skipping meals
- Reading the paper, working, or going online while eating
- Insisting both of you have what one person wants
- Criticizing how one partner prepares food
- Eating in bed and leaving crumbs
- Using one utensil in several dishes (mixing foods by using the same spoon in the gravy and mashed potatoes or jelly and peanut butter)
- Burping, nose blowing (or worse!) during a meal
- Licking food off fingers
- Not using proper etiquette (wrong fork, elbows on the table, wiping mouth with a hand or sleeve)
- Smoking while eating
- Eating with his or her hands
- Continuing to use a dirty napkin instead of grabbing a new one
- Taking food off your plate without asking
- Not washing hands before eating
- Taking phone calls during dinner
- Coming late to the table—after the food is cold
- Mispronouncing foreign food names or unusual ingredients
- Drinking from the milk or juice carton
- Slacking and not washing fruit/veggies before eating/ preparing them

- ◆ Overcooking food
- ◆ Using the same cup for everything without rinsing it out (i.e., soda right after milk)
- ◆ Over-seasoning food
- ◆ Rinsing or wiping but not washing cups/utensils before putting them back
- ◆ Double dipping
- ◆ Making noises or faces while eating

HOW TO TALK SANELY ABOUT THE FOOD HABITS THAT DRIVE YOU CRAZY

There is a simple process for resolving food nuisances. It's all about how you bring up the issue and what context you put it in. A common pitfall is to complain about something only in the heat of the moment. Effective communication requires a non-emotional, big-picture talk. Believe it or not, your partner may not be aware of what he or she is doing or have no clue how much a behavior annoys you. I have to admit that I was shocked when my husband told me how much it irritates him when I use his car and forget to readjust the seat and mirrors. What was a "no-biggie" to me was an ongoing annoyance to him, but because he never mentioned it, I was in the dark and kept right on doing it.

S T E P

Tactfully Bring Up the Problem

Find the right time to come forward with your concerns. Try to find a time when you and your partner will have ample time to talk, will not be interrupted, and are relaxed (see How to Protect Your Diet on page 63). Keep the tone light and humorous and limit your concerns to your top three to five annoyances. When you begin the conversation, start out with at least one positive thing your partner does in the food department, such as make the coffee every morning. Then, gently follow this with your top food pet peeve without attacking or judging. Finally, don't assume that your parter is already aware of the problem, even if you've mentioned it before—he or she may have tuned you out, not taken you seriously, or forgotten.

For example, consider starting out like this: "Bob, I love the fact that you make me soup when I'm sick, but there are a few things you do that really drive me batty, like when you leave the toaster out on the counter and put the ice cube tray back in the freezer when it's empty. I know it might seem silly or trivial to you, but it would really mean a lot to me if we could resolve these things."

S T E P

Hear His or Her Side

Listen carefully. Then ask for honest feedback from your partner about what you do that annoys him or her. Don't dish it out if you can't take it. And remember to always remain respectful and calm.

S T E P

Meet in the Middle

This is where the **N** in **SANITY** comes in. Use the negotiate **SANITY** step and compromise. To be truly willing to solve a problem, you have to be willing to negotiate, compromise, and agree to give and take a little. The beauty of compromise is that neither person has to completely surrender to the other. Offering your partner a compromise will help him or her warm up to adjusting how he or she does something. Choose one to three specific behaviors you'll each work on now that you're each aware they bug the other.

Catch 'Em and Kid 'Em

Step four may surprise you. The **Y** in SANITY, you'll recall, stands for **y**uck it up and use humor. Keep each other on task by yucking it up and using humor. Humor is a surprisingly simple and effective way for couples to relate to each other. Partners often share a sense of humor and know exactly how to make the other laugh. Tapping into that intimate connection can help you communicate better, personalize the solution to your problem with your own unique sense of comedy, and find the conflict resolution that will really work for both of you. I have more to say about this in Chapter Thirteen, page 145, so for now, let's say you consider adopting a funny phrase you utter when you catch your partner engaging in the annoying act. Instead of huffing, "You said you weren't going to do that anymore," take a deep breath and say, "Gotcha." Consider other fun activities or incentives to help you reach your goals. For example, the partner who gets snagged talking with his or her mouth full must give the other a foot rub, do the laundry, or put one dollar in a jar. Or, when you catch your partner in the act, use a gesture—walk over and gently tug his or her ear, or give him or her a big hug before reminding 'em they slurped coffee again. If you catch them when they aren't home, leave a friendly note on the fridge or send them a quick email that says, "You owe me a foot rub." It's essential to remember, though, that changing bad habits doesn't happen overnight and extend the patience and humor you'd expect to receive from your partner. And don't forget to thank your partner for successfully working on and changing his or her behaviors.

Expressing sincere gratitude is the best strategy for positive reinforcement and open communication.

Always keep in mind that these issues really are minor in the grand scheme of things. After all, no couple is spared at least a few quirky behaviors that irritate each other. It just so happens that some of these irritable quirks involve food and eating. Similar food foibles can be found between siblings, parents and kids, roommates, close friends, and even coworkers. If you find yourself feeling really bent out of shape over a food pet peeve, ask yourself if that's what you're really angry about. It could simply be the straw that broke the camel's back versus the specific behavior itself that's getting to you. The coworker whose insistent gum snapping drives you crazy is probably disrespectful in a number of other ways that have nothing to do with food. So, before you blame your partner's moldy leftovers for the demise of your relationship, take a deep breath and a step back. Sorting out a symptom from a real problem can help you solve food annoyances quickly and in a satisfying way, allowing you and your partner a chance to focus your energies on more serious matters.

2

You're Not Supposed to Eat That!

WATCHING WHAT YOUR PARTNER EATS—
BUT IN A HEALTHY WAY

 **It's 8:00 P.M.** and, as usual, Zoë, six months old, needs attention. Her mom, Carrie, thirty-one, is wrestling with her, trying to figure out what she needs first. She's hungry, fidgety, and she's grabbing Carrie's hair. Carrie's happy to tend to her little butterball; she's just a little tense and tired. After breast-feeding, Zoë burps and coos, happy and satiated. While Carrie clears her husband's dinner dishes, she decides she could use some comfort food herself. She's juggling the baby and a box of Hostess cupcakes when her husband, Dylan, walks in and shakes his head.

"I don't understand why you just don't have more willpower," he says.

It takes all of Carrie's willpower to refrain from smashing the cream-filled cakes into Dylan's face. Instead, she stuffs her own and quietly sulks. Can't he see that she's doing the best she can? Sure, those last fifteen pregnancy pounds haven't just melted off, but considering that she hasn't had any time to work out, it could be a lot worse. Pre-baby times feel like light-years ago. Before they were married, Carrie and Dylan couldn't sit still. They spent weekends mountain biking and rollerblading and made regular weeknight visits to the gym together. "Now," Carrie laughs, "I'm lucky if I get to take a shower!"

Carrie knows that Dylan means well, but his constant comments about her weight are just making the situation a million times worse. Every time she picks up a fork, he reminds her, subtly or harshly, that she said she'd lose the baby weight by now. His attitude has made meals uncomfortable, and, Carrie complains to her friends, "I'm beginning to feel guilty about eating anything!" Recently, she's been eating less in front of him and more when she's alone or with Zoë. A part of her wants to show Dylan that she can get back into shape, just to prove him wrong, but another part is resentful that he thinks it's so damn easy.

Carrie's sister Jenny suggested she meet with the registered dietitian that helped her after she gave birth. Dylan also thought it was a great idea but that made Carrie a little reluctant. She didn't want some militant dietitian taking Dylan's side. But she warmed up to the idea when Jenny explained I wasn't that kind of dietitian.

Carrie had a lot of feelings to resolve. First and foremost, she was feeling judged, which can be very painful. Overwhelmed by the sudden responsibility of the baby, she was angry and defensive because she thought she had a good excuse for gaining weight. Carrie also felt like Dylan should be loving and supportive regardless of her weight. She wants his help desperately, but his food cop behavior made her resentful. Carrie wanted to be treated like an equal—but that was difficult. The extra pounds lowered her self-esteem, making her more vulnerable and sensitive than usual.

One of the most common food fights I hear about has to do with one partner monitoring and commenting on everything that goes into the other one's mouth—those are the signs of a food cop. No one likes being policed, and yet we often do it to people we love in the name of "their best interests." In the quest to help a partner stay healthy, a food cop can become obsessive, overbearing, and in short, a tyrant. And as anyone who's ever been policed by a spouse will tell you, it almost never works!

Men do it, women do it, and it annoys everyone who's at the receiving end. Without question, food cops really do mean well and are "only trying to help." But instead of helping, food cops hurt. When a husband or wife becomes a food cop, the other person feel restrained, deprived, and treated like a child. Then human nature kicks in, and rebellion strikes. Spouses under surveillance sneak forbidden foods, hide eating habits they fear will be chastised, lie about away-from-home eating, and even binge when a precious opportunity to pig out arises. This can introduce other eating problems such as erratic and secretive eating, which can aggravate health problems like diabetes, hypoglycemia, and high blood pressure.

There's a fine line between helping your partner eat healthfully and driving him or her insane. A constant barrage of do's, don'ts, and food reminders can easily drive anyone crazy. But from the inside, the problem isn't always easy to see or fix, especially if you haven't learned the tools. The good news: talking about this problem will help you understand each other better. The SANITY model can eliminate problematic misunderstandings.

Here we're looking specifically at **S** (see the problem honestly) and **N** (negotiate). You have to honestly see a problem and negotiate to banish a food cop. It's not realistic to simply let go of the strong feelings you have about your partner's health (or vice versa), but you can learn to compromise. And even the person being patrolled probably wants some amount of help.

It's not all that fun to be a food cop, either. Food cops tend to be problem-solvers who take on a lot of responsibility. Often, they are worriers who are very concerned about his or her loved one becoming ill. A partner's health is of primary importance and takes precedence over everything. Other food cops are very self-disciplined with food and have a hard time relating to people who aren't. Eating well or staying slim is easy for them so they don't understand overeating or eating without hunger because it's foreign. But it's burdensome for one person to be responsible for the health of two people.

Couples like Carrie and Dylan need honesty to openly discuss how they got into this situation. Specifically, they need to talk about the feelings surrounding the situation, taking into account the language and tones used, as well as the frequency and timing of comments. With honesty, they'll be able to negotiate the terms of support, and turn a food cop into a food friend.

WEIGHT FOOD COPS

Although there are two kinds of food cops—weight food cops and health food cops—they are dealt with in the same way. Weight food cops like Dylan don't "get" their partner's relationship with food. To them, food is simple. A weight food cop is often very self-disciplined about food without being obsessive. Other weight food cops harbor bad feelings about those who are overweight. He or she may think being overweight is a sign of weakness or laziness and he or she just cannot understand how someone could just "let themselves go." This type of food cop might be frustrated that people with a weight problem can't just understand that if they want to be thin, they can't eat donuts.

Resolving the Weight Food Cop Problem

If weight food cops can understand the role food plays in their partner's life and relate it to their own personal coping mechanisms, they will see how food can be a comfort. For example, some people may use music or alcohol or sleep or sports to deal with stress. But many people have learned to use food to cope. When food becomes a tool that serves a purpose, it's not easy to just stop. Once a food cop understands this, it can help him or her see things in a new light. The food cop may see that comments like, "Just put your fork down," is like saying, "Don't call your best friend when you need to vent." Once they make that breakthrough in perception and understanding, the food cops will be able to resist asking, "Why can't you just stop eating?" and cease being critical. Of course, the other partner will need to explore and discover his or her own problematic food issues.

Weight food cops will also have to learn and accept the ramifications of their food cop attitude and behavior on their spouse. Unlike *health* food cops, who operate from fear and concern, weight food cops usually operate from misunderstanding. They must learn about their partner's relationship with food so they can stop hurting and start helping.

But first, the victim of the food cop has to take stock of the entire situation. Food was giving Carrie several things she lacked—comfort, instant gratification, a treat, and a break. She wanted to lose the weight but she may not have been ready to give up those benefits. Or, she might have been so overwhelmed that she just didn't know where to begin. Carrie's first step was to figure out how to explain her feelings to Dylan and then tell him what support she does and does not want from him.

This exercise got her started, and I recommend it if you're dealing with a food cop or you know you have a tendency to be one.

THE FOUR QUESTIONS
ABOUT FOOD AND FEELINGS

1. What troublesome words or phrases does your partner use in reference to your eating habits? List a few.
2. How does each of them make you feel?
3. Why do you think your partner uses these words and what is he/she trying to convey?
4. How would you have liked him/her to have communicated his/her intentions?

Let's look at how Carrie filled out the questionaire:

1. What troublesome words or phrases does your partner use in reference to your eating habits? List a few.

The words Dylan uses that bother me the most are "willpower" and "restraint." I don't like it when he points out certain foods I'm eating and reminds me that I "shouldn't" be eating them if I want to lose the baby weight or makes comments about the amount I eat. He'll say, "Do you need to be eating that?" It's what he says but also the way he says it that really gets to me. It's degrading. I feel like I'm two inches tall or a little girl who's being scolded by the teacher.

2. How does each of them make you feel?

When he uses words like these, I just want to punch him! It seems so easy for him to "restrain himself" but he doesn't know what it's like for me. He has no idea how tired I am and that I barely know what day of the week it is! My whole life has changed since Zoë came along. I guess I feel angry, and also judged, rejected, and guilty. I want him to help, but the exact way he phrases things and the tone he uses sometimes just make me feel both hurt and angry. Sometimes I want to cry and other times I want to clobber him!

3. Why do you think your partner uses these words and what is he/she trying to convey?

Maybe Dylan just doesn't get it. It seems so easy for him to eat when he's hungry and stop when he's full. He has never had a "thing" with food and I guess a lot of guys don't. I think he is trying to help but he doesn't understand that it's not as simple as he makes it seem! I want his help and support but the way he's going about it is making things worse.

Right after I had Zoë, I'd ask him to motivate me because I'd complain about wanting to fit back into my pre-pregnancy jeans, but what a mistake that turned out to be. Now I just want him to leave me alone!

4. How would you have liked him/her to have communicated his/her intentions?

I wish Dylan could just be me for a day! I think if he really understood how I felt he could empathize better. I don't want him to think I'm lazy or that I don't want to do it. I wish he could back off the judgmental wording, acknowledge how I'm feeling, focus less on my weight, and ask me what he can do to help me. For example, helping more with Zoë or around the house could really take some of the burden off me. If I had a little more time to myself I wouldn't need to be shoving food in whenever I can and maybe I wouldn't feel like I need chocolate to de-stress. I'm so self-conscious now I don't even want to get undressed in front of him. We used to take showers together. Now I lock the door.

After Carrie read her answers, Dylan said, "I had no idea I was making you feel that bad. Hearing this makes me feel like a monster!" He went on to say that now he can see why she's been less affectionate and cold.

"Well yeah," Carrie explained. "Every time we hug I feel like you're sizing up my weight."

After this session, we then invited Dylan into the conversation and asked him to take the following "Are You a Food Cop?" quiz. You can complete this quiz, too.

Are You a Food Cop?

FIND OUT BY taking this simple quiz. Or, if you think your partner may be guilty of food cop behavior, ask him or her to complete it. Please consider each statement about food and your partner and answer yes or no as honestly as possible.

1. I am very aware of what he/she is eating when we are together.

   Yes   No

2. I ask him/her what he/she eats when we are not together.

   Yes   No

3. I scold my partner for eating certain foods.

   Yes   No

4. I snoop around to see what and how much he or she has eaten.

   Yes   No

5. I regularly discuss his or her eating habits with other people.

   Yes   No

6. I try to influence what or how much my partner eats.

   Yes   No

7. We argue about his or her eating habits.

   Yes   No

8. I have tried to trick my partner into eating differently.

   Yes   No

9. The words "You really shouldn't be eating that" have come out of my mouth.

   Yes   No

10. I spend too much time and energy worrying about what my partner eats.

    Yes   No

Scoring

If you answered yes to any one of the questions, you're in the food cop academy. You haven't graduated to a full-fledged food cop yet, but if you don't watch it, you may turn into one. If you answered yes to more than two of these questions, you are probably a food cop. Another way to find out is to ask your partner to take this quiz from your point of view. Compare answers and discuss the results. You may view your words and behaviors differently than your partner. This exercise will give you an opportunity to openly discuss the issue, improve your communication, and enrich your relationship.

Not surprisingly, Dylan scored in the food cop range. Carrie used her four question answers to explain her feelings to him, and we started talking about the motivations behind his behavior. To help them both figure out how he can truly be supportive, we started on these tips. If you have any food cop tendencies, you can follow them, too.

HOW TO STOP BEING A FOOD COP

In just four simple steps, you can start curbing food cop behavior.

S T E P

Try to Avoid Judgmental or Negative Language

Being supportive is important, but nagging creates defensiveness and actually inhibits your partner from changing. Offer occasional gentle reminders and be mindful of judging. To avoid making it about "good" or "bad" behaviors, try not to use a critical tone and avoid saying the following:

- ◆ You shouldn't
- ◆ That's bad for you
- ◆ Don't

To find out which words or terms bother your partner, ask him or her to answer the Four Questions about Food and Feelings and review his/her response with you. Note to cop: You'll be pleasantly surprised to see how much further you'll get with "I just read that oatmeal is helpful for lowering cholesterol," than "You really shouldn't be eating that for breakfast; remember your cholesterol!"

S T E P

Don't Push too Hard

One of the things I've seen over and over again in my health care career is how strongly people resist being forced to do anything. When someone is scolded or aggressively told what to do (or what not to do), they tune out, get defensive, or get angry. It's human nature to dismiss nags. After all, as full-grown men and women, we don't like to have too many restrictions placed on our personal freedoms.

For example, when doctors send patients to see me, these new clients rarely come in smiling. Their tense body language, stern expressions, and stiff tone tell me they aren't happy. And they usually get defensive because they fear I'm going to lecture them and ban their favorite foods (which, of course, I don't do). This attitude is vastly different from clients who schedule an appointment because they truly want to be there. They smile and joke, genuinely enjoying our time together because they chose to see me. No one else can create that ready and willing attitude—it has to come from within. Forcing change on people who aren't ready for it only creates cynicism, and pushes them further away from healthy behaviors.

There's a much more effective way to gently encourage change that never fails to open my clients' eyes. Role-playing helps them share their points of view in a clever, interesting, and objective way. The exercise literally allows them to walk in each other's shoes and appreciate where their partners are coming from. This is another tactic that utilizes SANITY's honesty step. In a role-play, partners "switch skins" to adopt each other's body language, tone, and wording. After partners role-play for about five minutes, they can discuss their responses. Role-playing can be cathartic for both partners, and offers a gentler way to initiate honest communication and clarify feelings.

At first Carrie and Dylan were embarrassed to role-play but I assured them many couples find it helpful. I encouraged them to get into character by taking on the posture, body language, and voice of the other person.

CARRIE AS DYLAN:

(Giggles at first but then shakes her head disapprovingly and points her finger.)

Carrie, why do you keep buying that junk? You know you're not going to lose weight if you keep chips and cookies in the pantry.

DYLAN AS CARRIE:

(Speaks in a breathy, hurried voice, assumes a slumped posture, and rolls eyes.)

Whatever.

CARRIE AS DYLAN:

Well, you told me you wanted me to help you and I'm just saying . . .

DYLAN AS CARRIE:

I'm doing the best I can. You don't understand!

They looked at each other, unsure what to say next. I asked them to both take a deep breath and relax. When asked, they admitted this was a typical food-related conversation.

I asked Carrie if she felt Dylan portrayed her accurately. When she said, "Yes and no," I asked her to elaborate. She explained that while those were the things she would say to him, Dylan did not portray the way she felt inside. Her "whatever" comment and eye rolling were not uncaring. They were a reflection of how overwhelmed and vulnerable she felt, and a reaction to his attitude. Whenever she craves support and affection, she often gets this judgmental attitude from him.

Dylan listened, turned to Carrie, and said, "I'm not trying to be mean, the last thing I want to do is make you feel bad. I just know that losing the weight is important to you and you don't seem to have the same energy and confidence you used to."

"I want your help," Carrie responded, "but I don't want you to make me feel bad about myself."

I suggested we try a different role-play. This time, Carrie played herself and I portrayed Dylan.

CYNTHIA AS DYLAN

Carrie, I know you want to lose the weight you gained during your pregnancy and I want to help. What can I do?

CARRIE AS CARRIE

The best thing you can do to help is help me find ways to take better care of myself. When you make comments about what or how much I'm eating it hurts. If I had more balance

I might be able to spend more time preparing healthier meals. Right now there are so many things demanding my energy that sometimes the only simple pleasure I have is from food!

Then the real Dylan put his arm around Carrie, kissed her forehead, apologized, and promised to figure out how to make it work better for her.

Want to Try Your Own Role-Play?

TO GET STARTED, try switching roles and discussing what to have for dinner.

While role-playing may seem like child's play, it can become deeply serious and emotional. Before starting, agree on a set of ground rules, including this one: Either partner can stop the role play at any time by saying a safe word you've agreed upon ahead of time. "Quit" is a good safe word.

S T E P

Focus on How to Improve the Quality of Everyday Life

People can't always wrap their brains around abstract ideas, like the prospect of having a heart attack at the age of forty-two. I've worked with overweight men who have considerable family histories of heart disease, along with high blood pressure, and high stress (four significant risk factors), yet they refuse to believe anything will happen to them. In this case, it's much more salient to focus on what impacts the person today. For example, point out how energetic they will feel after a light meal instead of what a fatty meal will do to their arteries and cholesterol levels. You might gently ask how he or she feels after eating heavy foods, lightheartedly saying, "Didn't you need the Tums the last time you ate that?" or, "A few times you've mentioned that you have more energy when we eat light, how 'bout we order something else?" Comments like these may help him or her link what he or she eats to how he or she feels. This approach is more likely to result in change, because these things affect him or her in the here and now, instead of influencing a future health risk perceived as improbable or too far off in the future to worry about.

The role-playing worked very well for Carrie and Dylan, so step three came naturally. They understood their problems and were ready to create solutions. I told Dylan it sounded like he was focusing more on Carrie's weight than on her day-to-day quality of life. He nodded, and I asked him to think about how he could change his messages to her. Since she'd asked him to help her create more balance, I asked him to think about how he could word things in a way that focused more on her as a whole as compared to her weight.

Dylan said he could say things like, "I know you're tired. Why don't we have a light dinner so you'll have more energy?"

As a result of all this, it was clear that Dylan was really starting to see the big picture and, as a consequence, Carrie's relief and enthusiasm were apparent. They were now sitting closer, holding hands, and smiling.

S T E P

Make It Easier to Follow Through with Healthy Behaviors

There are lots of things you can do in this regard. Buy ready-to-eat health foods and make them available in the house. Place a bowl of inviting apples and pears on the kitchen counter. Place fresh cut-up carrots and celery on a prominent shelf in the fridge rather than tucked away in the crisper. Offer to whip up a healthy dinner. Pack your partner a nutritious lunch. Find new healthy restaurants to try. Offer (but don't push) tasty but healthy snacks, such as whole-wheat pretzels with salsa or low fat microwave popcorn. Your partner may find these munchies a nice change from his or her usual chips or cookies, which could result in a self-motivated desire to expand his or her eating inventory.

For Carrie and Dylan, step four was about concrete strategies and resources. Together, we came up with a list of ideas that felt realistic for them.

Grocery shopping was stressful for Carrie because it tempted her to buy comfort foods, so Dylan agreed to take on more responsibility with the grocery shopping and keeping the house stocked with healthy prepared foods. Dylan and I put together the following healthy shopping list:

Healthy Eating Checklist
- ◆ hummus
- ◆ tabouli and carrot raisin salad
- ◆ pre-washed cut veggies bags of washed and ready-to-eat field greens for salads
- ◆ grapes
- ◆ cut melon and fresh fruit
- ◆ pre-cooked chicken breast
- ◆ lean deli meats
- ◆ soy products to add to a salad or stuff into a pita
- ◆ nonfat yogurt
- ◆ reduced fat string cheese
- ◆ crumbled feta
- ◆ soy milk
- ◆ spring water

Dylan agreed to try to reduce his use of negative or judgmental words. He was thrilled to find a way to help Carrie find her previous energy and Carrie finally felt she was receiving the kind of support and resources she needed.

Now we're particularly interested in the **T** in SANITY. Take advantage of outside resources. Resources refer to important aids that are often overlooked—things that can help you solve a problem. Many times outside or professional help is needed. I suggested they find a regular baby-sitter, recruit friends and family to help out with the new baby on a regular basis, and have Carrie join a mommy and baby exercise group to help her bond with other moms and increase her activity level. (See Chapter Eight, page 95 for more details.)

With four simple steps, Carrie and Dylan began to transform their communication style, relationship, and lifestyle. By opening up and cooperating they created solutions as a team. Too many couples accept food conflicts as a normal part of relationships. But it's good to remember that they don't have to be, and resolving them can improve many aspects of a couple's life together.

After our sessions, Carrie and Dylan continued to work on their communication. Carrie was no longer afraid to tell Dylan how she was feeling and he was more sensitive to her needs. Over a few months, Carrie lost the baby weight healthfully. Now that she has a new feeling of balance, energy, and confidence, she started taking Zoë on regular bike rides and strolling her around the neighborhood.

Carrie was ready for a change. But not all food cop victims are. Stephen, in the following story, needed to do more self-exploration before he could face the food cop in his life.

Stephen, forty-one, was about to take a bite of his steak when his cell phone rang. When he saw his mother's number, he answered immediately. His wife, Katrina, knew something was wrong. "When? Where are you?" Stephen said before he hung up, put his hands over his face, and turned to her. "My father had a heart attack," he said. "He's in the hospital in intensive care. We need to go."

As Stephen's father made it through surgery and transitioned into cardiac rehab, reality started to set in. Stephen is a dead ringer for his father, and each time they visited her in-laws, Katrina envisioned Stephen in his shoes: pale and weak, with surgery scars on his chest and leg, absent of the vigor he was known for. Katrina, forty-one, needed to do something to prevent her husband of seventeen years from suffering this way. In the next couple of months, she decided they should both eat better to avoid future health problems. Katrina read everything she could find about preventing heart disease. Then she started reading food labels and modifying recipes. Stephen, however, was not interested in changing his diet. Even though his doctor said he has high cholesterol and slightly high blood pressure, he hasn't adjusted his couch-potato lifestyle.

Each time she saw Stephen drown his potato in butter or found out he had pepperoni pizza for lunch, she'd freak. At first, Katrina just reminded Stephen about his family history of heart disease and encouraged him to make changes. But when he didn't budge, she got crazy. She scolded him, recited statistics from the American Heart Association and, Stephen says, "She nagged and nagged and nagged me about my bad habits." Now she's a full-on food cop, and the more she pushes, the more obstinate Stephen becomes.

These days, he dismisses absolutely everything Katrina says about anything with a wave of his hand. So she's trying a new tactic. She talked to her friends and got the name of a registered dietitian. Eager to hear that she's right and Stephen should stop eating all that fast food and red meat, she scheduled an appointment for both of them. Stephen knew his father's dietitian was very reasonable and he agreed to go only in the hope that this dietitian, me, would see how insane Katrina had become and talk some sense into her.

Stephen and Katrina's health issues are slightly different than Carrie and Dylan, but their food therapy goals are the same. They need to communicate in order to honestly explain how and why they each feel the way they do and determine a new set of communication rules.

Health food cops like Katrina want to do anything and everything possible to keep loved ones healthy, so he or she tries to convince the partner to change their eating styles. Health food cops really believe his or her role is one of protection. Making a partner eat better is simply the "right thing to do." It's hard for them to understand that there's anything wrong with controlling or nagging actions. He or she doesn't see the problems caused by food cop behavior and believes he or she can convince the partner to do things better.

The biggest thing that health food cops do not understand is that their partners are responsible for their own behavior. There is nothing that Katrina can do to force Stephen to change. Katrina doesn't comprehend that he may not be ready to change, that he may not want to change, or that he doesn't take the risks of not-changing very seriously.

RESOLVING THE HEALTH FOOD COP PROBLEM

Health food cops are so focused on their mission, they can appear irrational. The food cop of a person who's had a heart attack, for example, may seriously think that one unhealthy meal will send his or her spouse to the emergency room. Ironically, they do not see the harm in their own actions. To solve this problem, it's crucial that they recognize the negative impact that food cop behavior has on the relationship.

The person who's being patrolled needs to better understand why their partner is acting like a food cop. They must empathize with their fear and concern. And the food cop must come to terms with the idea that he or she may not be able to change her partner's attitude, and then drop the dictator act and adopt a supportive one. Most likely, their partner will be willing to make some changes (though probably not as many as his or her partner would prefer).

In a case like this, it's important to address each person's feelings and actions, before we look at the couple as a whole.

Stephen's Side

When asked why he's here, Stephen acknowledged that he could make some dietary changes. He knew cutting back on desserts and soda could help improve his health, and he was somewhat motivated to reduce his cholesterol and blood pressure, but he thought Katrina was being way too militant.

Katrina's Side

But Katrina saw things differently and often overshadowed Stephen's point of view. For her, the time is now. She can't understand why Stephen doesn't make changes when he can see why and how to make them.

The walls put up between partners due to food policing impact their relationship as a whole. Not only can couples stop communicating with each other about food, they can stop communicating all together. The resentment and anger that builds between couples when one polices the other can get ugly. I've counseled several clients whose partners withheld sex because they were so angry that their significant other was breaking the food rules. Nipping food policing in the bud can rebuild communication, trust, and intimacy between partners.

A big part of this problem is that: wanting to change, even knowing how to change, does not mean a person can or will change. In addition to know-how, behavior change generally requires four steps:

1. Being ready
2. Being able to identify the obstacle(s)
3. Figuring out what you can use to help you change
4. Figuring out what you'll need to maintain the change

While Katrina is clearly ready to change her habits, Stephen isn't. Let's take a closer look at what's going on in Stephen's head through the following "self-assessment" assignment:

Stephen's Self-Assessment

I asked Stephen to answer the following questions to give me some insight into his current food-related feelings. You can complete this worksheet on your own, too.

WHAT'S YOUR ATTITUDE ABOUT CHANGING YOUR EATING HABITS?

- ◆ How do you feel about your current eating habits?
- ◆ In your words, what are the pros of changing your eating habits?
- ◆ What are the cons?
- ◆ Have you thought about making a change in your eating habits?
- ◆ If yes, what made you consider this?
- ◆ What gets in your way of making changes in your eating habits?
- ◆ What would need to change for you to consistently make and maintain healthy eating habits? Include anything that comes to mind.

At our next session, I asked Stephen to give permission to Katrina to read his answers.

- ◆ How do you feel about your current eating habits?

   I know they're not great but I don't want to change right now. Especially the 180-degree change Katrina wants. I know I need to eat healthier and I will but I have so much going on right now. I just need to do it in my own time.

◆ In your words, what are the pros of changing your eating habits?

I'm sure I'll feel better and probably lose weight and it will get Katrina and my doctor off my back.

◆ What are the cons?

It's just so much work. I don't want to have to think about all of that. It's like adding one more responsibility on the stack. I'm trying to figure out how to pay my daughter's college tuition and I'm worried about my job security. It's just not a priority right now.

◆ Have you thought about making a change in your eating habits?

Yes, but I put it off.

◆ If yes, what made you consider this?

I'm getting older. I mean, I can't believe my daughter will be in college. Sometimes I don't feel as old as I am! I know I need to start taking better care of myself but that feels like admitting that I'm getting older. I hate that.

◆ What gets in your way of making changes in your eating habits?

Stress, lack of time, and I'm sick of hearing about it. The more she nags me the less I want to do anything.

◆ What would need to change for you to consistently make and maintain healthy eating habits? Include anything that comes to mind.

> *How about winning the lottery! A personal assistant would be nice. If I didn't have to think about it so much I'd probably do better. The easier the better.*

Answering these questions helped Stephen take an honest look at his feelings and readiness to making changes. The process helped Stephen point out what's in his way, clarify his feelings, and figure out what he needed to make the change happen. In searching for a way to prompt dialogue with Katrina, he used The Four Questions about Food and Feelings exercise on page 12 to help convey his feelings to his wife.

The Four Questions exercise, however, was especially difficult for Stephen, which makes sense. After all, Katrina and Stephen have been together for a long time—their dynamic is more established than Carrie and Dylan's, for example—and they've had some food conflicts and food cop issues in their lives for several years. Because of the built-up resentment, it took longer for Stephen to get past his anger and resentment to identify the hurtful language. We can all learn from Stephen's process: some people will need to slowly tackle one question at at time while others can finish a whole exercise in one sitting. Be patient and do as little or as much as you can. Just work on them regularly.

Because The Four Questions exercise was especially difficult for Stephen, I supplemented it with a creative one. Here's the **I** in **SANITY**—imagining creative solutions. Imagining solutions is about thinking outside the box to find new solutions to old problems. Often times, lifestyle changes are difficult because we've been doing things the same familiar way for so long. Creativity helps you change perspective, view the problem in a new way, and open new doors to the answers you're looking for.

If one or both partners remain defensive, sometimes they get stuck in the same argument. The following exercise is great for overcoming stubbornness helps pull out the pent up feelings that are hard to put into words. Some find this exercise is easier to do because you work on it alone and then share.

At a Loss for Words?

WITH A PENCIL and paper, draw a picture that represents how your partner makes you feel about this situation. Exchange drawings and discuss.

When Katrina and Stephen completed the "At a Loss for Words?" exercise, Katrina had drawn a stick figure of herself with a sad face and one arm reaching toward Stephen, who was turned away, facing dark clouds, and Stephen sketched himself in a prison cell with Katrina outside, dangling the key.

This was a good way for Stephen and Katrina to break free from their stubbornness. Stephen was touched to see that Katrina was saddened by his situation, and that made it easier for him to start a dialogue. Katrina was shocked and sobered by the seriousness of Stephen's picture. Both were surprised by what came out of their artwork.

Eventually, all of these exercises helped Stephen communicate with his wife. By reviewing Stephen's answers and drawings with him, Katrina was able to see that Stephen wasn't just being obstinate. "I can't believe how much I oversimplified this," she said woefully at the end of the session. "I never knew how much is involved with change."

Amazed to see just how much her food policing hindered Stephen's progress, she was ready for some tips of her own, and eagerly approached the How to Stop Being a Food Cop steps on page 16. Less than two months later, she'd worked through them all, and had overcome her food cop tendencies.

Stephen started following through with his behavior changes. He made small changes at his own pace and set his own—not Katrina's—goals. First, he cut back on red meat, then started eating a healthier breakfast, and then added more vegetables to all his meals.

Because Katrina backed off, Stephen could focus on what he felt good about changing instead of what he "should" change. He gauged his success and set new goals based on the rewards he was getting from the changes he instigated. Because he had more energy, was sleeping better, and suffering from less heartburn, he sincerely wanted to keep making healthier changes.

3

Why Won't You Just Try Some?

HOW A PICKY EATER CAN MAKE PEACE WITH AN ADVENTUROUS ONE

 Stephanie, twenty-seven, and Mike, twenty-eight, have lived together for two years. Her simple tastes have always differed from his. She likes grilled fish or chicken with rice and veggies, lasagna, McDonald's fries, chicken Caesar salad, pasta with marinara sauce, Frappacinos, and, well, that's about it. She can literally count the number of foods she'll eat on two hands. Since their first date, Mike has always compromised to eat her way. They usually eat her favorite dishes at home or go out to one of the three restaurants she likes.

Lately, Mike has grown tired of sticking with Stephanie's food program. At heart, he's an adventurous eater who craves new flavors, textures, and spices. He's dying to check out a new Middle Eastern place that opened up near their house, as well as a famous Thai restaurant close to his office. The most "ethnic" thing Stephanie eats is Chinese—but only chicken and broccoli, with the sauce on the side. She's not interested in expanding her food horizons and is perfectly content eating the same thing every day. Feeling disappointed, frustrated, and hungry for some culinary excitement, Mike came to me for advice.

Mike and I work together, and one afternoon he casually told me about his dilemma. We were in the lounge and I had just come back from the deli with blackened tofu, couscous, and grilled asparagus.

Intrigued by my lunch, he asked, "Does your husband eat that way?"

"Well," I laughed, "he's willing to try new things but this wouldn't be his first choice."

"At least he'll try," he said, and went on to explain how Stephanie's monotonous menu was really getting to him.

Mike had three options. Firstly, he could continue to compromise and find alternative ways to satisfy his cravings. Secondly, she could change. Or lastly, they could meet in the middle. I asked if Stephanie knew how he felt.

He hadn't brought it up but mentioned that they've always had good communication. "I'm sure she'd be willing to talk about it," he said. "But I don't think there's a solution—we're just so different when it comes to food."

Mike approached Stephanie with the following worksheets and asked her, "Remember when we had trouble getting the mortgage and we worked through it? Well, I need your help again. Would you be willing to set aside some time to fill these out?" You can complete these questionnaires, too, and follow Mike's gentle approach to talking with Stephanie.

Picky Eater's Questionnaire

QUESTION	RESPONSE
How do you think your partner feels about your differing eating styles?	
How do you feel about your differing eating styles?	
Do you think your differing eating styles have caused problems in your relationship? If yes, please explain.	
Are you willing to make any changes in your eating style? If so how often? If not please explain.	
What are the advantages and disadvantages of compromising your personal eating style?	

Adventurous Eater's Questionnaire

QUESTION	RESPONSE
How do you think your partner feels about your differing eating styles?	
How do you feel about your differing eating styles?	
Do you think your differing eating styles have caused problems in your relationship? If yes, please explain.	
What changes or compromises in your personal eating style have made since entering into this relationship? Please explain.	

These worksheets foster the **s** step in the **SANITY** model—seeing the problem honestly—as well as communication. They help partners find out how each other feels and how much each is willing to compromise. Additionally, they also help couples determine if there's a gray area in between a black-and-white eating pattern.

After completing the questionnaires, couples switch papers or read their own answers out loud to each other. But first, it's a good idea to set some ground rules, such as these:

◆ No interrupting
◆ No raising voices
◆ No accusations
◆ No sarcastic comments

Exchange answers, and before reacting, take time to hear each other out. Think about what the other person is saying. By exploring each other's feelings, you can develop a reasonable plan of action without anyone feeling bullied, blamed, or disappointed.

Here are Stephanie's responses:

QUESTION	RESPONSE
How do you think your partner feels about your differing eating styles?	*I don't know. I never really knew it was a problem until he asked me to fill this out!*
How do you feel about your differing eating styles?	*Well, I know Mike likes more things than I do but I don't prevent him from eating what he wants.*
Do you think your differing eating styles have caused problems in your relationship? If yes, please explain.	*Well, obviously Mike feels it's a problem or he wouldn't have brought it up, but there are other things he likes to do that I don't, like play golf and he just does that with the guys.*
Are you willing to make any changes in your eating style? If so how often? If not please explain.	*I'm not sure. I'm just a picky eater. I've tried different things in the past and just don't like a lot of things. I've always been this way.*
What are the advantages and disadvantages of compromising your personal eating style?	*I guess the advantages are it would make Mike happy and we might get out of the rut we've been in of doing the same thing practically every weekend. The disadvantages would be that I really don't enjoy trying new things so it wouldn't be a lot of fun for me, and if I don't find something I like at a restaurant I leave still hungry because I'd rather not eat than eat something I don't like. This happened when we were on vacation in Mexico.*

And now Mike's:

QUESTION	RESPONSE
How do you think your partner feels about your differing eating styles?	*I don't think she's very aware of it. Sometimes I think she doesn't notice how I always give in to her preferences.*
How do you feel about your differing eating styles?	*It's frustrating! I like food and trying new restaurants and items is fun for me. I'm sick of eating plain pasta or grilled fish for dinner! I feel like I'm missing out on something I really enjoy.*
Do you think your differing eating styles have caused problems in your relationship? If yes, please explain.	*Yes. We end up going to the same few restaurants all the time so our weekend routine has grown boring. I'm not mad at Stephanie because I don't think she purposely tries to control our way of eating but the few times we have gone to places where she couldn't get her usual foods (like in Mexico), she either won't eat or she'll complain and either one kinda ruins the meal and the rest of the evening.*
What changes or compromises in your personal eating style have made since entering into this relationship? Please explain.	*A lot! I feel like it's just easier to defer to Stephanie since it's always been more of a problem for her to not get what she likes than for me to give up what I like. But, I feel like it's too hard for me to always give in.*

After Stephanie saw Mike's answers, she was very concerned and agreed to come in. At our first meeting, Stephanie expressed her worries, saying "I feel awful—I had no idea Mike felt this way. I don't want him to feel like he's missing out but I'm just picky—I can't help it! We don't know what to do."

"Stephanie," I replied. "You wrote that there are other activities Mike enjoys that you don't such as playing golf and he simply does this with the guys. Food is a little different because you two share about twelve meals a week and eating together is a way you spend time and socialize. The good news is there are compromises you can make that won't require either of you to completely give in to the other.

In general, a varied diet is good for everyone. It provides a wider variety of nutrients to the body. A limited diet can lead to a nutrient-deficiency. The vitamins, minerals, phytochemicals and antioxidants in food maintain our bodies and prevent disease. Taking a multivitamin will not come close to compensating."

Mike and Stephanie will benefit from the **N**, **I**, and **T** parts of the **SANIT**Y model. They can solve their problem by negotiating a compromise, imagining creative solutions, and taking advantage of outside resources.

HOW TO SPICE UP YOUR SHARED MEALS

Setting a few ground rules and thinking outside the box can help couples with different tastes compromise.

- *Take Turns*
  When dining out, alternate who gets to choose the restaurant or type of food.
- *Seek Out Variety*
  Dine at eclectic eateries that offer a big assortment. One partner can enjoy a traditional meal and sample the other's exotic appetizer or side dish.
- *Look Before You Leap*
  Before you go out, go online to view a new restaurant's menu or have it faxed over.
- *Think Outside the Entrée*
  Order three appetizers instead of two and do a sampling. The more you get, the more of a chance you'll end up with something you like. And the adventurous eater can pack up the leftovers for lunch.

◆ *Order Take-Out—Twice*

Pick up different foods from more than one eatery in the same vicinity. The new Ethiopian restaurant Mike has been eyeing may be right down the street from Stephanie's favorite grill. Call in your orders to save some time, head home, and enjoy being together while you both eat what you prefer. (Mike and Stephanie loved this suggestion. "I don't know why I never thought of that," he said.)

◆ *Bring Backup*

Stash a Plan B food, like a Power Bar, in case you can't eat the new food.

"It sounds like this is the worst case scenario: you try but don't find something new you like," I said to Stephanie. "Mike mentioned that when this has happened before it ruined your whole evening. When you try this again, try it with a new attitude as well as a backup plan. If you don't like your entrée, chalk it up to adventure and eat a Luna bar afterwards so you won't be hungry. Or, stop for a latte or other tie-over snack to get you through the rest of the evening."

"That's true," Stephanie said. "It's really not that big of a deal if I don't get one meal a week I like, and I never thought about the protein bar idea. I like Luna bars and I am definitely willing to try."

Here's where the **A** in the **SANITY** model comes in—ask your partner to understand the problem and support you. Mike's focus will be on asking Stephanie for support, as well as finding creative solutions. Generally, there are two ways a partner can support you. They can do something that directly helps you, such as making a healthy dinner when things get hectic. Or, they can do something that indirectly helps, such as buying a George Foreman grill so that you can make healthy meals more easily. The idea is simple: your partner can do lots of little things to make your lifestyle changes easier. Picking up the groceries or doing the laundry can really free time up so you can work out. The perfect acts of support are offered as needed and depend on the person and the problem, but they can be discovered with the food therapy processes described throughout the book.

HOW TO ENCOURAGE EXPERIMENTAL EATING

You can help a picky eater expand his or her eating repertoire by adopting a supportive attitude.

◆ *Tie One On:* An apron, that is.
   Offer to cook the same meal two different ways. For example, before marinating the chicken in curry, set aside your partner's portion, then spice yours to your liking. Share as many ingredients as possible, altering things in slight ways.
◆ *Do Lunch or Dinner with Friends*
   Set regular dates with those who share your love for spicy foods. Bring home the leftovers to share in a less pressured environment.
◆ *Offer Up a Bite*
   Ask your partner to try a little of your food instead of ordering an entire entrée. He or she may be surprised how unexpectedly delicious strange foods can be!

Now that Stephanie knows how Mike feels, she's willing to be more open. "I was just being myself but I can see now how it wore on him," she said. "I'm willing to try some of the stuff he enjoys."

Once an issue like this is uncovered, simply keeping your eyes open to the other's body language keeps the conversation going. This couple will find success if they continually touch base. Mike must be more vocal about his feeling so Stephanie is aware of the problem. Awareness, along with discussing progress periodically, will allow this couple to have fun and really enjoy eating together again.

 **Michelle, thirty-four,** is a pharmaceutical sales rep and a gourmet who studied cooking in France. She prides herself on her sophisticated palate and her knowledge of flavors, recipes, and wine. So it surprised her as much as everyone else that she married a "meat-'n-potatoes" man. Dan, a thirty-six-year-old accountant, grew up with an English mum who served very straightforward foods, like steak and eggs, meatloaf, and ham. Michelle's parents were true foodies. Her idea of a good time is spending a weekend preparing a civilized five-course meal. The problem: Dan is not impressed when she makes fancy food or experiments with new recipes. In fact, he doesn't like it at all. He refuses to eat garlic, a staple in her cooking, and often rejects the headliner ingredients. The other night, for example, she had to make "Steak sans Poivre" instead of "Steak au Poivre" because Dan found the pepper flavor too strong.

Michelle tries to keep a good attitude, but, she admits, "The joy kinda goes out of it when I bring out a new meal and he looks down at his plate, screws up his face, and says, 'What is this?'"

Michelle approached me at a health fair where I gave a cooking demonstration. She described Dan and his stick-in-the-mud food attitude. When I asked if there was any chance Dan might come around, Michelle shook her head. "I love Dan, he's perfect for me in so many ways, but he'll never be a foodie," she said.

We talked about food personalities and whether they're shaped by nature and nurture. Michelle offered an interesting anatomical theory about her husband: She suspects Dan was born with only two taste buds, instead of ten thousand!

In a situation like this, when there's virtually no chance for compromise, Michelle must go it alone. Her love of food is a huge part of who she is, and her ties to the world are very linked to it. When she's not cooking, she adores tending to her garden, browsing the farmer's markets, and reading the "Dining In/Dining Out" section of the *New York Times*. It pains her that she can't share this aspect of herself with Dan, but she's not willing to just ignore that part of her personality.

Most couples have this kind of problem, whether it's related to food or not. Sometimes one partner is passionate about baseball, capable of recalling every moment of the last five World Series, or the stats of every player on their favorite team. The other may not give a flying leap about sports. You can live without baseball, but you can't live without food. Unlike leisure activities, food is a daily necessity. Eating issues are a bit trickier.

Michelle can indulge in her gourmet interests without Dan. This involves taking advantage of outside resources, the **T** in **SANITY**. She can throw monthly dinner parties with foodie friends who will truly appreciate her culinary efforts, submit her original recipes to contests, or join a culinary group or wine club to meet others who share her passion. Michelle had thought about doing some of these things, but worried about making so many plans that didn't include Dan. This won't be a problem if she simply communicates her feeling to Dan before she fills up her calendar with activities that exclude him.

Does Michelle's situation sound similar to yours? Are you unsure of what to say? Here are some easy ways to explain the need for time apart:

- ◆ "As much as we have in common, there are some passions we don't share with each other."
- ◆ "It doesn't make sense for me to expect you to enjoy this just because I do."
- ◆ "I don't want to make you miserable by forcing you to do this with me."
- ◆ "I enjoy going a lot less when I know you can't wait to get out of there."
- ◆ "I know we're secure enough in our relationship to take pleasure in some separate activities, so I'd like to try to find ways of balancing our 'us' time with 'me' time."

- "Here are some ideas I came up with . . . (Then spell out the types of ideas you're talking about.) What do you think?"

Michelle listed some activities they could do together, as well as things she could do on her own. Here are her ideas:

"US" TIME

- Monthly dinner parties
- Have "experiment night" once a week. Make two versions of one meal: a basic, non-gourmet version without sauce or spices and another version with all the fixin's, i.e., a plain baked potato with butter for him, crème fraiche mashed potatoes for her.

"ME" TIME

- Teaching cooking classes
- Planning culinary trips with friends
- Submitting recipes to contests
- Joining a culinary group or wine club
- Taping cooking shows or buying Tivo to record cooking shows as well as Dan's favorite football and baseball games

To coordinate schedules, try meeting regularly to discuss upcoming plans. Pick a day of the week to sit down and compare notes. If it's too difficult to do that in person, try sharing a wall calendar at home, investing in Palm Pilots, or registering on a virtual calendar website so you can each post and view commitments online. Some good calendar Web sites include, www.supercalendar.com, www.myappointments.net, and www.ezintranets.com.

And don't forget to plan things together. Make planning as routine as buying groceries or doing laundry. If you're busy, schedule dates for movies, or concerts, or just TV time at home. Couples need a minimum of two to three quality dates each week, even if that just means taking a walk together or playing Scrabble. Parents can book a regular Tuesday night babysitter, even if it's only for an hour and a half. If money is an issue, see the mommy swap childcare solution in Chapter Eight, page 95.

Once they put their heads together, Michelle and Dan were even able to brainstorm activities that combined their separate interests. They planned trips to the bookstore café where Michelle could browse cooking magazines while Dan could check out the latest nonfiction. Dan's a sports fan, so Michelle suggested she catch up on her cookbook reading while he could take in a game at home.

The bottom line is that Dan doesn't love Michelle for her seemingly effortless ability to whip up a soufflé. He loves her for myriad other reasons and she has to be okay with that. Michelle may be used to receiving praise for her gourmet skills, and not getting this from her own husband may feel strange. But, if she accepts that this is not an essential ingredient in a healthy relationship, they can both maintain their distinctly different food personalities and live happily together.

4

Will You Be Home for Dinner?

FINDING TIME TO EAT BETTER TOGETHER

Family meals are a challenge, especially when small children are involved, and I will give advice about family food therapy in Chapter Eight. But first, let's tackle the meal schedule issues that come between couples.

 **Newlyweds Ann, twenty-four,** and Dennis, twenty-five, relish their time together, but don't have much of it. She's a teacher and he's a realtor so their schedules differ. Ann gets home several hours before Dennis. By the time she gets settled, she's starving and ready for dinner, but waits for him so they can rehash the day's events over a meal. Most afternoons, however, Ann ends up snacking to keep herself satiated. Because she's so hungry, carrot sticks, fruit, or rice cakes just won't do it. She ends up eating more filling foods like Oreos, Doritos, and Triscuits and cheese before she makes dinner. By the time Dennis gets home, Ann isn't really hungry but she eats with him anyway. As a result, she's gained a few pounds and feels sluggish and self-conscious.

When Ann visited me, she was disappointed in herself and feeling guilty. "I know what I need to do but I just can't seem to do it," she said. "I don't know what's wrong with me. I guess I don't have any willpower."

Willpower won't solve her problem, but smart meal timing will. Postponing meals is incredibly problematic for many people. It can lead to undereating, overeating, weight gain, fatigue, irritability, and mood swings. Denying the body regular fuel also aggravates medical conditions such as hyperglycemia or hypoglycemia, high cholesterol, and high blood pressure—so it's very important to time eating well.

Eating at the right time means coordinating hunger, the clock, and nutrition, and that's just for one person. Couples need to consider the hunger, schedule, and nutrition needs of two people.

Ann is well enough in tune with her body to recognize how hungry she truly is when she gets home from work. Many adults are out of touch with their bodies and unaware of what physical symptoms of hunger feel like. They eat when their watches or their emotions tell them to, often ignoring their bodies' needs. Our bodies and minds work *together* to help us decide what, when, and how much to eat as well as when to stop.

Think about how your body and mind work in concert. When you're in a cold room, for example, your body tells you it's not comfortable by giving you signals, like shivers or goose bumps. When your mind recognizes those signals, it tells you to find a way to warm up to a comfortable temperature. Your body tells your mind to put on a sweater.

When you're in touch with your body, you recognize and respond to your body's signals. But if you're disconnected from your body, you tune them out. Ignoring your body's signals is dangerous because you can hurt yourself. Ignore the signs of being cold and you may end up with frostbite.

When Ann gets home from work, her body is telling her it needs fuel. Her blood sugar is low because she's already burned through her lunch. Ann's body is ready to be refueled. If she ignores her body's signals, she'll eventually become overly hungry. Being too hungry inevitably leads to overeating—grabbing the first thing available, eating too fast and too much, and having a hard time determining when you're full. Ann's first goal was to prevent extreme hunger.

The following hunger scale helps people, like Ann, figure out when they're eating enough and when they're overeating:

Hunger Scale

-5 = out-of-control hunger (shaky, trouble concentrating)

0 = comfortably hungry (non-intense feeling of emptiness but no discomfort)

3 = physically full but not satisfied (still thinking about food)

5 = full (but not overfull), satisfied and energized

8 = uncomfortably full (feelings of pressure, slight discomfort, sluggish)

10 = painfully full (intense pressure or pain, need to lay down, take antacids, change into looser clothing, very sluggish)

Aim to stay in the middle of the scale. Eat at a −3 (when comfortably hungry) and stop at 3 (when you're feeling comfortably full).

Ann ranked her hunger for each waking hour. Then she plotted the times on this graph:

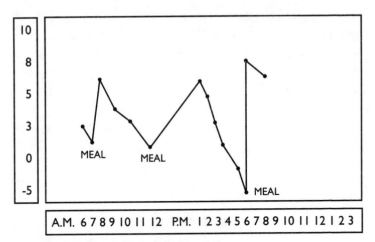

−5 = out of control hunger (shaky, trouble concentrating)
  0 = comfortably hungry (non-intense feeling of emptiness but no discomfort)
  3 = physically full but not satisfied (still thinking about food)
  5 = full (but not overly full), satsified and energized
  8 = uncomfortably full (feelings of pressure, slight discomfort, sluggish)
10 = painfully full (intense pressure or pain, need to lay down, take antacids, change into looser
      clothing, very sluggish)

Aim to stay in the middle of the scale. Eat at a 0 (when comfortably hungry) and stop at 5 (when
you're feeling comfortably full, satisfied and energized).

Ann was at a 0 before lunch and then a 5 after lunch, but
when she got home from work, she was at a −5. Ann was where
she's supposed to be at lunch but definitely not at dinnertime.

A well-balanced lunch typically provides four hours of fullness
and sustained energy. Because she was lunching at noon, there
were more than four hours between lunch and when she gets
home. If she waits until 6:00 P.M. or 7:00 P.M. for Dennis, she
goes five or six hours without a real meal.

When Ann gets home, her body is ready for a meal, which is
why just a piece of fruit won't do the trick. But she really wants
to eat dinner with Dennis.

Sharing meals is an important bonding experience, especially
for newlyweds. But when adapting your eating pattern to your
partner's causes physical and emotional problems, it's time to
find a better solution.

Well-timed and balanced meals will create a pattern where

Ann never dips below a 0 or rises above a 5. There are several options available, both to Ann and you:

COORDINATING DINNER

If you and your partner put your heads together and strategize, you should be able to find some alternatives to traditionally shared meals when your schedules clash.

1. *Start Your Meal Solo*

   Eat the entrée when hungry and then snack while your partner dines. Go ahead and have dinner and then enjoy a salad, soup, or even dessert while he or she eats. Or, split up the meal and consume the heartiest portions (the protein and starch parts) alone, and the salad or veggies with your partner.

2. *Sit Together, Eat Separately*

   Enjoy your dinner before your partner gets home and simply sit while he or she eats. Instead of feeling like you're giving up eating together, focus on the idea that you're spending time together, talking, and sharing the events of your day. Enjoy a cup of tea or lemon water.

3. *Snack Four Hours after Every Meal*

   One hundred calories provides enough energy for about one hour's worth of normal activity. If you have lunch at noon and dinner at 7:00 P.M., you'll need a three-hundred-calorie snack at 4:00 P.M.

4. *Snack Smart*

   An ideal snack offers complex carbohydrates, protein, fiber, and healthy fat. This combination keeps you fuller longer because protein and fat slow digestion. The best snack is filling enough to make you satisfied (5) yet not so heavy that you're still full by dinner. We've been taught that eating in between meals isn't good, but it really depends on the timing of your meals. Eat something at least every four hours. If your snack is well-timed and not too high cal, you'll still be hungry for dinner.

5. *Eat Breakfast Together*

When you can't coordinate dinner, carve out fifteen minutes in the morning to share coffee or go out to breakfast and catch up.

After evaluating her hunger scale and recognizing the importance of coordinating hunger, the clock, and nutrition, Ann decided to snack so she could wait for Dennis and have dinner with him. As long as she picked a healthy snack, she'd be able to tide herself over without spoiling dinner.

EATING IN SYNC HEALTHY SNACKS

Think of these foods as high-octane fuel. They deliver a lot of nutrients without a lot of preparation.

- ◆ One quarter cup walnuts or almonds mixed into eight ounces yogurt
- ◆ One half cup oat bran pretzels dipped into two tablespoons of peanut butter
- ◆ One string cheese strip and a small handful of whole grain cereal (like Cheerios or Bran Chex)
- ◆ One quarter cup soy nuts and one packet of instant oatmeal
- ◆ One ounce soy jerky or turkey jerky with a small handful whole grain crackers (like Carr's or Kavli)

- One medium apple, sliced and dipped into two table-spoons of peanut butter
- An energy bar with fifteen to thirty grams of carbohy-drate, ten to twenty grams of protein and five to ten grams of fat (Luna Bars, Cliff Bars, Mojo Bars, Kashi Go Lean Bars, Detour Bars, Genisoy Bars)
- One half cup edamame (whole soy bean pods found in the frozen or produce section of the grocery store)
- Two tablespoons peanut butter and a small handful of whole-grain crackers
- One cup celery or cucumbers with two tablespoons peanut butter or soy nut butter
- One quarter cup nuts
- One half cup pineapple chunks
- High fiber granola bar (with more than three grams of fiber)
- One half cup trail mix (without coconut or salt)
- Twelve-ounce skim latte
- One quarter cup dried fruits

See more eating in sync healthy snacks in Chapter Ten, pages, 120–121.

Seeing her problem honestly enabled Ann to imagine practical solutions. By incorporating well-timed healthy snacks into her day and rethinking how she eats with Dennis, Ann felt better imme-diately. As long as her diet remains consistent, she should lose the weight she has gained and easily maintain her normal weight.

 **Heidi, thirty-five,** and Richard, thirty-six, are two busy health care professionals who have lived together for almost five years. Neither has the time to shop for groceries, let alone prepare a meal. Heidi is a hospital administrator and Richard is a chemist, and both bring work home in the evenings. They

understand the importance of healthy eating, but try as they will, their typical take-out or order-in sites leave much to be desired in the way of nutrition. They end up eating chicken quesadillas, crab wontons, burritos, and other heavy meals with too few vegetables. Many days the only vegetables they see are the lettuce and tomato on sandwiches or turkey burgers. Heidi called me for advice and asked, "Can you help us eat better without cooking?"

Many couples like Heidi and Richard don't realize there are resources and tools that can make it easier for them to follow through with their goals.

Because both partners are on the same page and equally motivated, they're ahead of the game. They just need some tips and tools to help them get where they want to go.

"Time just gets away from us," Heidi said. "We have all these great intentions of making salads and grilled fish but we end up ordering Chinese. I know that's not too bad but you never really know what's in those sauces. We'd both like to have more control over what we're eating."

Couples with crazy schedules can learn a lot from analyzing their daily routines. The following exercise tracks exactly how time is spent—right down to every quarter hour. Try writing down what you do with every fifteen-minute period of your day. Track this for three days—two week days and one weekend day. Next to how you use your time, note possible alternatives. This column can be eye opening.

TIME TRACKER

TIME	ACTIVITY	POSSIBLE ALTERNATIVES
5:00—5:15 A.M.		
5:15—5:30 A.M.		
5:30—5:45 A.M.		
5:45—6:00 A.M.		
6:00—6:15 A.M.		
6:15—6:30 A.M.		
6:30—6:45 A.M.		
6:45—7:00 A.M.		
7:00—7:15 A.M.		
7:15—7:30 A.M.		
7:30—7:45 A.M.		
7:45—8:00 A.M.		
8:00—8:15 A.M.		
8:15—8:30 A.M.		
8:30—8:45 A.M.		
8:45—9:00 A.M.		
9:00—9:15 A.M.		
9:15—9:30 A.M.		
9:30—9:45 A.M.		
9:45—10:00 A.M.		
10:00—10:15 A.M.		
10-15—10:30 A.M.		
10:30—10:45 A.M.		
10:45—11:00 A.M.		
11:00—11:15 A.M.		
11:15—11:30 A.M.		

TIME	ACTIVITY	POSSIBLE ALTERNATIVES
11:30—11:45 A.M.		
11:45—12:00 P.M.		
12:00—12:15 P.M.		
12:15—12:30 P.M.		
12:30—12:45 P.M.		
12:45—1:00 P.M.		
1:00—1:15 P.M.		
1:15—1:30 P.M.		
1:30—1:45 P.M.		
1:45—2:00 P.M.		
2:00—2:15 P.M.		
2:15—2:30 P.M.		
2:30—2:45 P.M.		
2:45—3:00 P.M.		
3:00—3:15 P.M.		
3:15—3:30 P.M.		
3:30—3:45 P.M.		
3:45—4:00 P.M.		
4:00—4:15 P.M.		
4:15—4:30 P.M.		
4:30—4:45 P.M.		
4:45—5:00 P.M.		
5:00—5:15 P.M.		
5:15—5:30 P.M.		
5:30—5:45 P.M.		
5:45—6:00 P.M.		
6:00—6:15 P.M.		

TIME	ACTIVITY	POSSIBLE ALTERNATIVES
6:15–6:30 P.M.		
6:30—6:45 P.M.		
6:45—7:00 P.M.		
7:00—7:15 P.M.		
7:15—7:30 P.M.		
7:30—7:45 P.M.		
7:45—8:00 P.M.		
8:00—8:15 P.M.		
8:15—8:30 P.M.		
8:30—8:45 P.M.		
8:45—9:00 P.M.		
9:00—9:15 P.M.		
9:15—9:30 P.M.		
9:30—9:45 P.M.		
9:45—10:00 P.M.		
10:00—10:15 P.M.		
10:15—10:30 P.M.		
10:30—10:45 P.M.		
10:45—11:00 P.M.		
11:00—11:15 P.M.		
11:15—11:30 P.M.		
11:30—11:45 P.M.		
11:45—12:00 A.M.		
12:00—12:15 A.M.		
12:15—12:30 A.M.		
12:30—12:45 A.M.		
12:45—1:00 A.M.		

TIME	ACTIVITY	POSSIBLE ALTERNATIVES
1:00—1:15 A.M.		
1:15—1:30 A.M.		
1:30—1:45 A.M.		
1:45—2:00 A.M.		
2:00—2:15 A.M.		
2:15—2:30 A.M.		
2:30—2:45 A.M.		
2:45—3:00 A.M.		
3:00—3:15 A.M.		
3:15—3:30 A.M.		
3:30—3:45 A.M.		
3:45—4:00 A.M.		
4:00—4:15 A.M.		
4:15—4:30 A.M.		
4:30—4:45 A.M.		
4:45—5:00 A.M.		

One client I worked with found she spent a considerable amount of time talking on the phone, going online, and cleaning. When she added it up she was amazed. When she cut back a bit on phone and Internet time and hired a part-time cleaning service, she freed up a considerable amount of time for shopping and preparing healthy meals.

HOW TO SQUEEZE HEALTHY MEALS
INTO A TIGHT SCHEDULE

It will take some forethought, but there are lots of simple ways to boost the nutritional value of the types of meals you're already eating.

◆ Make a weekly trip to the market a standing commitment by building it into your schedule. Give this the same level of importance and priority as a work-related appointment or meeting. Your grocery list should include these Eating in Sync Healthy Items:

   1. Frozen veggies you can quickly reheat to balance out heavier take-out meals. Microwaved broccoli spears, spinach, green beans, or asparagus can be quickly seasoned with black pepper, lemon juice, balsamic or red wine vinegar, or herbs to provide a light and healthy compliment to a small portion of heavier take-out food.

   2. Pre-cut veggies like pre-shredded carrots and zucchini, pre-washed fresh spinach, pre-cut red and green pepper strips, pre-chopped broccoli florets, and pre-sliced mushrooms can be added to take-out entrées. They'll slash the percentage of calories and fat per bite, add crunch, variety, nutrients, and fiber. Find them in the produce aisle.

   3. Calorie-free beverages such as water, non-caloric flavored water, or Crystal Light. Dropping caloric beverages is one quick and easy way to balance out your calorie intake.

   4. Preserved fruits like dried fruit, frozen fruit, and fruit canned in natural juice are not nutrition no-nos. When you're on the run, even peeling an orange or washing a fresh apple can feel like too much of a time sacrifice. Stock your briefcase or desk with dried apricots, raisins, cranberries, plums, or figs for a quick and easy way to fit in a serving of produce. Pack the office fridge with canned pineapple or unsweetened applesauce. One quarter cup of dried fruit, the size of a golf ball or one half cup or four ounce canned are the equal to about one cup fresh fruit.

◆ Add produce to take-out/order-in meals. Request extra vegetables on pizzas, sandwiches, subs, and wraps. Add an order of steamed broccoli, coleslaw, or a salad. Throw your prepared veggies into rice, pasta dishes, sandwiches, pitas, or other take-out meals.

◆ Expand your take-out order. Order from more than one restaurant to create balanced meals. Instead of getting fries as a sandwich side, ditch the fries and grab a second order of vegetable stir-fry (sans rice) or vegetarian soup from a Chinese, Thai, or Indian eatery nearby. Ethnic restaurants offer wonderful veggie side dishes and salads that can favorably round out your meals. All it takes is an extra phone call.

◆ Have groceries delivered or order your fruits and veggies online. Many grocery chains provide grocery delivery services. In fact, some Web sites display each and every store item with the Nutrition Facts labels. Other delivery services exclude frozen or fresh items, offering only dry goods. Remember, even canned vegetables (rinsed to remove excess sodium), and canned or dried fruit is better than no produce at all. For home delivered healthy goods, check out:

1. www.peapod.com
2. www.netgrocer.com
3. www.freshdirect.com
4. www.groceryshopping.net

5. www.harryanddavid.com

6. www.ethnicgrocer.com

7. www.justtomatoes.com

◆ Hire a personal food shopper. Nowadays, many successful adults employ personal trainers and assistants,
pet sitters, private clothing consultants, and even life
coaches. A personal food shopper can be a real investment in your health, quality of life, and everyday pro-
ductivity. It's also an investment in your future because
it can help prevent disease. A shopper can stock your
kitchen with ready-to-eat items such as fresh salads,
cut vegetables with low-fat dips, fresh fruit and fruit
salads, and bottled water. To find a personal food
shopper near you, contact a personal chef in your
neighborhood who might provide the service or refer
you to someone who does. You can also consult
www.personalchef.com/findmain.htm.

After reading the above list, Heidi said, "Wow, I never would
have thought of these. I think we needed something like this to
get us going. Now I see so many possibilities."

Couples like Heidi and Richard have a conflict with the clock,
not with each other, so the SANITY ideas that apply to them are
asking each other for support and taking advantage of helpful
resources. Heidi and Richard need to support each other to
keeping eating well a priority. Work has ruled their time for a long
time, making it easy to slip back into old patterns, like skipping
a trip to the grocery store. This couple needs each other to stay
on track and prevent that from happening.

They can take advantage of outside help by finding professional resources to assist them, like the online shopping directo-
ries or personal shoppers. When they filled out their Time
Tracker sheets, they found that a lawn service would help
Richard free up the time he spends on yard work. It also became

clear that an accountant could help them manage the time spent on finances.

I know that a lot of you may think that these services seem expensive, but they are investments in your health. Poor diet leads to costly chronic diseases later in life, so you'll save on doctor bills, prescription drugs, and physical therapy down the road. And all the extra energy you get from eating well is worth it.

A body, like a car, needs regular tune-ups and maintenance. Most people believe that maintenance prevents car trouble and that ignoring problems is just asking for engine damage. But they don't take care of themselves as well. Many people schedule maintenance for their homes, lawns, and pets but many don't maintain their bodies. Eating well is the foundation for good health, so scheduling a nutrition tune-up once or twice a year is key. It's helped many of my clients, like Heidi and Richard, stay on track with nutrition goals, weight maintenance, and life changes.

I continue to see Heidi and Richard a couple times a year, and each time they are eating even better. They now understand that they can accomplish all of their health-related goals by supporting each other, reaching out, and getting yearly nutritional "tune-ups."

5

But It's Not the Same Without You

HOW TO STOP YOUR PARTNER FROM SABOTAGING YOUR DIET

From the very start of their relationship, eating was recreational for Diane and Tom. They spent the first three years of marriage splitting pizzas, sharing hot fudge sundaes, and bowls of buttered popcorn. Then Diane turned forty and got serious about eating right. It was harder to stay in shape, and as more relatives got sick, she focused on preventing diabetes and the other chronic diseases that were part of her family history. Diane, a social worker, loved the energy that came with eating well and was enthusiastic about her commitment to health. Tom, forty-two, was less than thrilled. He missed their old way of life and wasn't interested in swapping spanakopita for salads. Diane said she wasn't asking him to change if he didn't want to.

"But it's not the same without you," he'd say, and do everything he could to undermine her efforts.

He dismissed her diet and purposely tempted her by bringing home her favorites: donuts, fresh olive bread, and warm bagels. Diane saw this as sabotage, and Tom's lack of support took a toll on their relationship. She wanted his encouragement and understanding, even if he didn't share her newfound joy in eating healthfully. Diane confided in a close coworker who had recently attended I lecture I gave about making healthy changes work for families. The next day Diane called.

Many couples face this problem. When one half of a couple changes his or her diet and the other does not, havoc often ensues. Tom, or anyone in his position, may feel that cherished dining routines have been abruptly abandoned. What, when, and where they eat together has changed and usual entrées, favorite restaurants, and regular grocery items are not acceptable to both of them anymore. Eating patterns they've shared for years vanish overnight, and this can be a big adjustment for the partner of the person initiating the change.

Believe it or not, this is the primary reason many healthy eating plans and diets fail. The tension and lack of communication is why many people aren't successful in sustaining lifestyle changes. Giving up is easier than fighting. After trying to stand your healthy ground, you cave, and end up guilted or bullied into taking a bite of your partner's cheeseburger or ice cream cone. So long slimmer waistline . . .

In Diane and Tom's case, he may feel unsteadied by her sudden change in eating habits, and any change can lead to anxiety or resentment. By bringing home breads and bagels Tom not only resists eating healthy, but also tries to convince Diane to give up her healthier lifestyle. If Diane doesn't address this with Tom, the situation could snowball.

"I don't know if he'll talk about this," she told me. "He can be pretty stubborn and it's like he's taking this personally." As I mentioned in Chapter Two, when words fail, visuals can often break through stubbornness and jumpstart a conversation between partners. Look at this triangle:

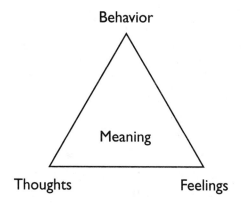

Behaviors are linked to thoughts, feelings, and underlying meaning. Diane felt unhappy about how she'd been treating her body. Her thoughts came from how her eating habits made her feel, and from how her diet was influencing her long-term health. So, she changed her eating behaviors. The underlying meaning behind Diane's change in behavior came from her desire to take better care of herself and take charge of her health.

When a person does or does not do something, it's often because of unrecognized thoughts and feelings. This triangle encourages *honesty* and makes it easier to see what's motivating behavior.

Diane took the triangle home, and prepared to discuss her feelings and viewpoint with Tom.

HOW TO PROTECT YOUR DIET

Communication is the best defense. How you present your point of view is just as important as what you say. Be mindful of tone and try to explain that this is not just about you.

◆ *Set the Stage*
    Schedule a quiet time to sit down and talk. Choose a place where you won't be interrupted.

◆ *Explain Your Motivations*

Help your partner understand your point of view and try to better understand his or hers. Be prepared to thoroughly explain why you decided to make these changes and thoughtfully express how meaningful they are. Your partner may not fully understand why you are doing this.

◆ *Focus on His or Her Feelings*

Ask how the changes you've made make him or her feel, not just what he or she thinks about them. Thoughts and feelings are different. Understanding both will help you put actions into perspective.

◆ *Hear What He or She Is Saying*

Listen without reacting too quickly or getting emotional or defensive.

◆ *Ask for Help*

Once you open up to each other and start talking, ask if your partner is willing to work on this issue. See if he or she will come in for a nutrition consultation together or complete other exercises as a team.

When Diane and Tom sat down on the patio for their scheduled meeting they opened a bottle of wine and toasted to a Saturday evening alone. Diane showed him the triangle. Tom looked blank.

She resisted the urge to shout out of frustration and took a deep breath. Referring to the triangle, she explained the thoughts and feelings behind her change. "Hitting forty had a big impact on me," she said. "I'm starting to think that every headache, sore muscle, and bump is bad news. I saw my mom struggle with her health. She didn't take care of herself and she paid the price. I don't want to have to inject myself with insulin or go through quadruple bypass."

"I know, honey. I'm sorry." Tom's face softened. "It's just that all of a sudden *you* decided to make this change and I have to deal with it, like it or not."

"What do you mean?" she asked.

"Well, I'm not trying to be unsupportive, but you know, our whole routine has been wiped out. It's like we were in the same place, we had these comfortable habits, the cookouts, Papa John's and Marble Slab on Friday nights, brunch on Sundays . . . it's like a huge part of what makes us 'us' has suddenly changed. I miss the old Diane."

"I had no idea all that was so important." Diane was genuinely surprised. "I mean, we'll still have our routines, but different routines. I just don't want our lives to revolve around food. I know it's fun, believe me, but when I think about what I want more, I want my health. I want to feel good."

"Diane, these past three years have been so wonderful," Tom sighed. "I guess I just feel like you're leaving me behind. I want to grow old with you and it's like you want to stay young."

"Tom. I love you! I have no intention of leaving you behind. I want to grow old with you, too, but I just want us to be healthy old people!" She put her arms around him and squeezed tight.

The triangle helped illuminate the thoughts and feelings behind Tom's behavior. He thought Diane was abandoning him, and that made him afraid, so he sabotaged her diet. The underlying meaning came from a desire for stability in their relationship.

Tom's entire attitude was changing and he was interested in really tackling this problem. They tried other recreational activities, like antiquing and mini golf, that did not involve food. Tom was now supportive of Diane's changes, but he wasn't quite ready to completely adopt all of her healthy habits.

"I want to work toward changing too but not at warp speed," Tom said.

Tom and Diane had achieved honesty, and the next goal on their list was to learn how to negotiate and compromise. These following basic tips will help them, and you and your partner, start on a journey to a healthier life together.

HOW TO SUPPORT A PARTNER'S DIET WITHOUT FOLLOWING IT

You don't need to actually go on the diet to support a dieter, but there are some small steps you can take to make things much easier for him or her.

- *Personalize Your Portion*
   Instead of sharing a pizza, order two small ones so each person can customize their order, i.e., thin crust with veggies versus the works. Enjoy his and hers popcorn bowls while you watch a DVD. Fill one with light microwave popcorn, the other with regular popcorn and melted butter.
- *Skip the Economy Size*
   Buy a few donuts, not an entire box. If one wants donuts, he or she can purchase single portions instead of tempting the other person with a box full of leftovers.
- *Make the Food Court Your Home Court*
   The mall has a great variety where one partner can have a Big Mac while the other orders a wrap or grilled chicken salad.
- *Share Time, Not Meals*
   If one partner wants to go out for ice cream, the other can come along without indulging. Enjoy an icy diet soda and the time together instead of a cone.

Healthy eaters like Diane can learn to live with their partner's indulgences. Resist temptation by changing your mind-set.

RESISTING TEMPTATION

Try not to label food in terms of good or bad. When you place foods off limits, you'll be more drawn toward them. Instead of thinking of something as bad or unhealthy, ask yourself, "Is this something I'll really enjoy?" Then decide if it's worth it. If it is, enjoy it, savor it, relax, and eat until you're satiated. Then stop, knowing it's not your last chance.

When you don't put foods on a "no-no" list, you won't feel threatened, tempted to overindulge, or compelled to get enough before it's taken away. Trust that as an adult, you have control over your food intake, and can always meet your needs. Allow your hunger and satiety signals to guide you instead of relying on willpower, or a strict eating regiment. This will make it much easier to say, "no thanks" when offered an ice cream cone or a slice of piping hot pizza.

The next time you feel tempted, ask yourself:

◆ What is my body telling me?
◆ Is this what I really want?
◆ Will this food satisfy me?
◆ If I don't indulge will I feel deprived? If so, why? Is my reasoning rational?
◆ When will I have another opportunity to enjoy this particular item?
◆ How am I going to feel after I eat this food?
◆ Is it worth the indulgence? If not, am I really missing out?

 **Jessica, a twenty-seven-year-old** teacher, and Robert, twenty-nine, a real estate lawyer, met on match.com. Things moved quickly and, about a year after their first date, they got engaged.

Eager to say, "I do," they set a wedding date only six months away. They efficiently booked a hall, photographer, band, and florist. As soon as Jessica found a dress, she started the Atkins diet. She knew other brides who had dropped two to three dress sizes on the low-carb diet and she was determined to do the same.

Before they were even married, the honeymoon ended. They began bickering and each time Jessica fell off the no-carb wagon, she blamed Robert for eating bread and sugar in front of her.

"Jess went from a fun-loving low maintenance girl to a bread-phobic bridezilla!" Robert told his friends.

"Everyone goes a little nutty before a wedding," Jess said. "It's a big day, and there's going to be two hundred guests watching me. That dress is sheer. I can't hide myself in a tuxedo like him."

They fought constantly.

"Jess, all of a sudden, you latched onto this diet thing like it's life or death," he said. "I know you're stressed out but now you're irritable and tired all the time and that can't be healthy."

"You just don't understand, Robert," Jess sighed. "This is my wedding day."

"It's my wedding day too," he retorted.

Jess just wanted to look as good as she could. She knew a high protein diet wasn't super healthy, but felt it was only temporary. The honeymoon was in Fiji, and ten days in a bikini and a sheer wedding dress justified the diet.

"I just want to look good for you," she said.

"No, you want to look good for you," he said. "I think you look beautiful now and I'd rather have a healthy fun wife than an underweight crabby mannequin."

Getting married is one of life's most stressful events, right up there with serious illness and losing your income. Jessica and Robert were, understandably, on edge.

Unbalanced diets of any kind, high protein or low protein, cause physical and emotional side effects. Increased cravings, irritability, and fatigue are at the top of the list. Jessica was suffering from digestive problems, low energy, and headaches. In her state, tensions can easily erupt into arguments. Plus, being restricted from certain foods she loved—like carbs—was taking an emotional toll, on both her and Robert. "Every once in a while I breakdown and I just wish you wouldn't eat cookies in front of me—it drives me crazy!" she'd say.

Carbohydrates, in particular, are our preferred fuel source because they are the most chemically compatible for the human body. When deprived of carbs, the body must switch fuel systems, and burn whatever it can to meets its energy needs, including dietary protein and fat. If the deficit is great enough, the body will resort to burning muscle tissue, stored fat, and stored carbohydrates. This causes physical and emotional stress.

Jessica knows she probably won't keep the weight off and will continue to feel tired and cranky, but it's still worth it to her. Her comment, "We're going to have those pictures for the rest of our lives!" sums up her perspective.

Clearly, Jess and Robert have different view points. Jessica believes that since the diet is only temporary and feeling good about her body on her wedding day is so important, she wants to stick with it. And she'd like Robert to be supportive.

Robert, on the other hand, feels that Jessica's diet is unhealthy, unnecessary, and causing more harm than good. And he resents that she is asking him to give up cookies and change. But mostly, he wants her to stop worrying about her weight so much and just be herself.

Jess and Robert are an example of a couple that needs to negotiate and *compromise* to solve their food conflict. But compromising isn't always as easy as being honest. This exercise can help them and you.

Spell Out Each Partner's Argument

CREATE A LIST of pros and cons. On one side of a piece of paper, write down why you should do what your partner wants you to do. On the other side, write down why you're doing what your doing. Then read the list aloud.

Robert wrote "Reasons to Support Jessica's Diet" on one side of a piece of paper and "Reasons to Convince Jessica to Stop the Diet" on the other.

Jessica wrote "Reasons to Take Robert's Advice" and "Reasons to Defend My Diet Choice."

Robert read his "Reasons to Convince Jessica to Stop the Diet" list.

- ◆ Because I don't think it's healthy and I don't want her to be unhealthy.
- ◆ Because I can see that it's causing her to not act like herself and I want the old Jess back.
- ◆ Because we're already stressed out and the diet is adding one more stress to our lives.

His "Reasons to Support Jessica's Diet" said:

- ◆ Because I love her and want her to be happy on our wedding day.

Jessica read her "Reasons to Defend My Diet Choice" list:

- ◆ Because my wedding day is one of the most important days of my life and I want to look beautiful.
- ◆ Because the diet is only temporary.
- ◆ Because it's quick and easy.

Then her face softened and she read her "Reasons to Take Robert's Advice."

- ◆ Because I don't want to add to our stress right now.
- ◆ Because he loves me and is just trying to take care of me.
- ◆ Because I trust him.

Jessica and Robert exchanged a warm look.

Sometimes before partners can compromise, they need to see each other's point of view.

Jessica decided that she would work with me to loosen up her diet so she could still look and feel good for her wedding. Her first assignment was to think about the ways she needs Robert to be supportive. After we created a more balanced eating strategy for Jessica, she made a list of "too tempting" foods—these are foods that she is trying to avoid. It will be easier if Robert doesn't eat these foods in front of her or keep them in plain sight. She immediately knew what she would put on the list: cookies, ice cream, Chipwiches, any baked good or dessert, and Robert's homemade sangria. Robert said he'd be willing to eat those foods when he wasn't with Jessica, at least until she felt comfortable enough to add them back to her eating plan.

Dealing with Alcohol Issues

WHEN ONE PARTNER cuts back on alcohol for weight control or health reasons, and chooses to avoid alcohol-related activities, it can affect the social life of the other partner. If the partner who drinks can't find a way to be supportive or becomes intensely emotional about this change, it may be an indication that he or she has a drinking problem. For more information, visit the National Institute on Alcohol Abuse and Alcoholism and the National Clearing House for Alcohol and Drug Information's Web sites:

www.niaaa.nih.gov/publications/booklet.htm
www.health.org/govpubs/ph317/

The next time Jessica starts a new diet, she can save herself and Robert some grief by preparing him in advance.

PREPARING FOR A DIETARY CHANGE

Before you abruptly make a change, spell out the what, why, when, and how for your partner so he or she knows exactly what to expect.

- ◆ Explain to your partner why you want to make this change. Include the health benefits (such as losing weight, having more energy, preventing disease) along with the relationship ones (less focus on food, more time to enjoy other fun activities). If you're making a change because of a new diagnosis, be sure to read about how to recruit your partner's support in Chapter Twelve .

- ◆ Think like your partner, predict his or her reaction, and prepare your responses to those points ahead of time. Keep in mind that as well as your know your partner, you never can tell exactly what another person is going to do.

- ◆ Choose the right time and place to talk to your partner. Avoid distractions from others, noise, and time constraints.

- ◆ Set a date to execute the change. Agree on a good time and use the transition period to reduce tension by talking about and preparing for the change.

- ◆ Point out exactly what will change and what won't, i.e., meal timing may stay the same but the type and quantity of food may differ. Specifically explain any aspects of your eating routine that will be affected, including dining out, weekend and vacation eating, holidays, and grocery shopping items that you may not want in the house anymore.

◆ Be realistic and think the change through. You should be confident that the goal you've chosen is reachable and will result in positive versus negative short-and-long term health outcomes.

WHEN YOUR PARTNER IS GEARING UP TO GO ON A DIET

Try not to take your partner's dietary change personally, but at the same time, recognize that any change he or she makes directly affects you.

◆ Be completely honest about your true feelings about the change. Express them thoroughly and thoughtfully without getting emotionally combative. If necessary, take a few days to think about your feelings and write them down and set a second date to discuss them with your partner.

◆ Listen to the reasons why your partner wants to change his or her eating habits and try to see the positive effects it will have on your relationship.

◆ Take a few moments to reverse roles and see things through your partner's eyes. It may help you to understand where he or she is coming from. You should be able to verbalize the reasons for the change from his or her point of view.

◆ Remember the last change you made that was supported by your partner, and consider the importance of that support. Think about how difficult it would be for either of you to make an important change without the other's help. Focus on how the strengths of your relationship have counterbalanced challenges in the past.

Another SANITY principle that applied to Robert and Jessica's problem was imagining creative stress solutions. Neither of them had significant tension outlets. Jessica talked to friends and her mother, and Robert played basketball, but they were still stressed out.

They, like you and your partner, will both benefit from creating some new ways to relax. Here are some suggestions:

HOW TO RELAX IN LESS THAN FIFTEEN MINUTES

Everyone should try to work a little relaxation time into each day. Stress release plays an important role in immunity and good health. Chronic stress can lead to illness or a longer recovery if you get sick or injured. These ten simple acts can immediately invigorate you and truly benefit your life (and your partner's life) in the long run:

1. *Catnap*

   Set your alarm to go off in fifteen minutes and lay down. Let yourself go, knowing you don't have to watch the clock and those fifteen minutes are all yours.

2. *Zone Out*

   Listen to a guided meditation CD while sitting in a comfortable chair or lying down. Tune into the voice on the CD, letting go of any thoughts related to tasks or responsibilities. Meditation CDs are available on www.gaiam.com.

3. *Get a Professional Service*

   Take time out for a shoe shine, a shave, or a brief chair massage. You may not have the time or funds for a vacation or a full day at a spa, but a regular fifteen-minute professional treatment can do wonders to ease tension.

4. *Let Your Imagination Carry You Away*

Take a five-minute mini-vacation by practicing visualization. Choose where you want to go. Close your eyes and use all of your senses to re-create the sights, sounds, smells, and surroundings. Bring anyone with you you'd like to quietly sit by your side and share the view. Visualize a sprawling beach, a green mountaintop, an open field, green forest, or even an underwater scuba scene.

5. *Hit the Showers*

Take a relaxing warm bath or shower. Progressively relax each muscle group from your feet to your face and allow the warm water and steam to loosen and sooth your muscles.

6. *Steal a Scene*

Pop in your favorite DVD and advance to your favorite part. Laugh or cry and allow yourself to be swept away from your everyday life for just a few minutes.

7. *Dive into a Book*

Read a chapter or listen to fifteen minutes of a book on tape each day. Prop your feet up, sip warm tea or a cool refreshing drink and allow yourself to be taken away. It's a mini escape you'll look forward to each day. Not sure what to pick up next? Browse the bestseller list or the staff favorites at your local bookstore.

8. *Take a Deep Breath and Stretch*

If you relieve the tension in your back or your legs, your whole body will feel better. Use a door handle to destress your shoulders: With the door propped between your feet, pull the knob with both hands, bend your knees and slowly round out your back. A bathrobe belt can do wonders for your hamstrings: Sit on the floor with your legs out in front of you, wrap the belt around the soles of your feet. Keeping your back straight, pull the belt as you lean forward.

9. *Commune with Nature*

Spend fifteen minutes interacting with any living thing other than a human. Cuddle with a pet, feed ducks at a pond, tend to a garden, water the lawn, watch the clouds roll by, or gaze at the stars.

10. *Be a Kid Again*

Grab a box of crayons and construction paper and go to town. If crayons don't cut it, find another creative outlet: play video games, knit, write a poem, or start a craft project.

These are just ideas. Do whatever works for you, but do something. Taking time to relax often gets pushed to the bottom of the priority list when we're busy, and it takes work to keep it a priority. Stress is like a balloon, the more ways you find to reduce it, the easier it is to keep it deflated. But if it builds and builds, it will eventually pop.

For many couples, communication is the ultimate de-stressor. Looking at things through each other's eyes keeps the communication lines open and stress levels low.

By taking advantage of my nutrition advice (an outside resource) Jess and Robert were able to share their points of view and negotiate a compromise quickly. Once they took those positive steps, they used creative stress outlets like gardening and renting funny movies to take pressure off themselves and their relationship. The couple not only enjoyed the wedding planning more, but they were able to truly enjoy their actual wedding. With her moderate diet Jess shed enough weight to feel confident in her dress and bikini but still maintain her energy level. And they both lost the relationship tension they'd been carrying around, which made for a happy honeymoon indeed.

6

Eww . . . What Is That?

BRINGING TOGETHER DIFFERENT REGIONAL
AND CULTURAL EATING STYLES

 **Lauren, twenty-five,** moved to a suburb near Dallas, Texas when her fiancé Billy, twenty-six, relocated for a better job. Originally from the northeast, she grew up eating pastas, wraps, salads, seafood, perogies, and many vegetarian entrées. Billy, however, grew up in Texas and is a downhome southern boy. He was raised on chicken fried steak, meatloaf, mashed potatoes with cream gravy, fried okra, beef brisket, spicy peppers, and hot sauces. Billy loathes many of Lauren's favorite foods. Beyond being unfamiliar, he thinks they are unappealing and unsatisfying.

"That would never fill me up!" he says, dismissing her food.

The local grocery stores and restaurants don't carry many of the foods Lauren is used to. She is distraught at the notion of having to cook separate meals when they eat together. "Even dining out is difficult," she says. "I can hardly ever find anything I like on the menus here."

Lauren and Billy are like most people. Their food preferences are part of their cultural upbringing, a defining part of who they are as individuals. Dietary preferences are part of what makes you "you." They're not just about food, they're about the history of your life, your interaction with the environment, your family, your culture, and your memories. In short, food preferences are about what tastes like "home."

====
====

Why Moon Pies and Deep-fried Twinkies Are an Important Part of Any Healthy Diet

FOODS THAT REMIND you of home hold a special place in your heart and your diet. If you're away from home, make it a point to eat them occasionally to stave off homesickness and nurture your food personality. Clients from all parts of the country have passionately told me and other ADA spokespeople about how important it is to keep the following foods in their lives:

- ◆ Pittsburgh Clark bars and Primanti's sandwiches
- ◆ Coney Island hot dogs
- ◆ Philadelphia Cheese steaks and Frank's Black Cherry Wishniak soda
- ◆ New York bagels, pastrami sandwiches, and pizza
- ◆ Tennessee Moon Pies and RC cola
- ◆ Texas biscuits and gravy, fried okra, jalapeño corn bread with butter, Blue Bell ice cream
- ◆ Louisiana pralines, turtle soup, red beans and rice with mustard greens
- ◆ Florida key lime pie, Cuban sandwiches, black beans with yellow rice, stone crabs
- ◆ Cincinnati chili
- ◆ Cleveland chicken paprikash and Euclid Beach popcorn balls
- ◆ Milwaukee beer bread
- ◆ Chesapeake crab cakes

- Santa Fe cornbread
- Vermont maple syrup
- Indiana corn chowder
- Kansas City BBQ and baked bean casserole
- Arizona enchiladas and mesquite-flavored meats
- Georgia peaches, pecans, Mayfield Farms ice cream
- Southern deep-fried Twinkies and grits

It's completely unrealistic to expect either Billy or Lauren to adopt the other's way of eating. Luckily, there are ways for couples like them to live together without either giving up his or her unique food personality.

Because Lauren has recently moved, she must find ways to make peace with food in her new environment. Lauren has a few options. With the support of friends, family, and outside resources, she can connect to her roots. If you are in a similar situation, here are a few helpful hints to get an occasional taste of home:

HOW TO MAKE PEACE WITH FOOD
IN A FOREIGN LAND

Once you acknowledge that regional foods are important to you, it's just a matter of wrapping your lips around them regularly.

- *Ask for Care Packages*

   Friends or family back home will probably be happy to send your favorites. A college client of mine who attended school over one thousand miles from home was deeply homesick. As a treat, her family sent locally made ice cream, packed with dry ice, and literally made her day. Lynn, a wonderful friend of mine who lives in my upstate New York hometown, periodically sends me my favorite candies from the local shop. She finds pleasure connecting friends and family to their roots. She also sends her Wyoming-based relatives locally produced soups, sauces, and other goods they can't get out west. Care packages can prevent you from feeling isolated in a foreign food environment.

◆ *Order Regional Foods Online*

Many grocery chains offer online ordering and shipping. With today's technology, you may not have to do without. If you can't find what you're looking for, call a store in your hometown and see if they'll ship to you if you order online or via phone. Lots of e-shops cater to regional food lovers seeking local flavor. Search for your favorite foods or specific region on a search engine or browse the goods offered on these Web sites:

www.hometownfavorites.com
www.the-golden-egg.com
www.vermontcountrystore.com
www.tastygram.com
www.homesickgourmet.com
www.foodlocker.com
www.purelyamerican.com
www.cajun-shop.com

◆ *Make Regular Trips Home*

Nothing beats relaxing at your favorite hometown spot, ordering familiar food, feeling right at home, and leaving fully satisfied. After moving across the country, one of my clients experienced an incredible craving for soft frozen custard. She sat down with the phone book and called every ice cream and dessert place trying to locate her favorite treat. Many of them had never even heard of soft frozen custard, and she was heartbroken. I recommended watching out for airfare specials and grabbing a deal when she saw one. A few months later she was enjoying the real thing while catching up with some old friends. This trip allowed her to feel more at peace with her new environment. While it may sound trivial, foods-of-origin are extremely significant. Every once in a while, make it a priority to go home for the real deal. And while you're there, ask your favorite places if they ship or distribute near you.

As Lauren finds ways to adjust, she and Billy can explore the negotiation tips in Chapter Two and Chapter Six, pages 69–70. As you start to compromise, it may feel strange to eat together without eating the same thing. It's more than worth the effort. When Lauren and Billy came to terms with the fact that she would never love jalapeños and he would never like clam chowder, they were able to let go of this issue and direct their energies elsewhere. Lauren and Billy's new Friday night routine is dinner and a movie. They dine at the food court where he can enjoy Kenny Roger's Roasters with coleslaw, baked beans, and a biscuit and she orders a slice of Sbarro pizza with Caesar salad. Their newfound compromising skills have spilled over into other areas of their relationship. They take turns choosing the movie each week and alternate which family they spend the holidays with.

 **Brian, fifty, is a CEO** who often speaks publicly, so his appearance is important to him. He's always watching his weight. But his forty-six-year-old girlfriend, Emily, makes that difficult. She's second generation Asian American. She grew up eating a lot of rice, and serves it with every meal. Brian, an Irish American who grew up in Pennsylvania and then moved to New York City, loves rice but tries to avoid the carbohydrates. Oddly enough, he had a similar problem with his previous girlfriend, Francesca, an Italian American, who cooked pasta all the time. He didn't handle that situation well. When he tried to tell Francesca that the pasta was problematic, he put his foot in his mouth by saying, "Does your family have to eat pasta with everything?!?" Francesca interpreted his comment as an insult

to her family and the tension around family meals and holidays remained until they broke up. I met Brian at a party, and he asked for advice about how to discuss cultural differences in a sensitive, politically correct way.

I've seen similar tensions when one partner is kosher or follows a specific diet for religious reasons. Usually, the best way to deal with this issue is to talk and learn more about the cultural or religious diet. Understanding the traditions or thinking behind an eating style can help you get to know your better half better.

Before Brian could immediately dismiss Emily's cultural staples, he needed to sit down with her for a cultural culinary lesson. That way, she could explain what various foods are made of, how they are prepared and eaten, and their cultural significance. Understanding the place these foods have in Emily's heritage can help Brian see beyond how they impact his weight. If this story sound familiar, talk to your partner about making healthy compromises at home. He or she will probably be much more receptive to, "I'd like to try a healthier version of this," than "I won't touch this because it's way too fattening."

HEALTHY ETHNIC CUISINE

A number of cookbooks recreate ethnic cuisine using healthy ingredients. Cooking from these books can be a great way to explore healthful versions of your partner's foods while you learn more about his or her traditions. Try devoting an evening to experimenting with a variety of dishes which you can then freeze, eat during the week, or defrost at a meaningful moment.

◆ *Secrets from a Healthy Asian Kitchen,* by Ying Chang Compestine

◆ *Healthy Asian Vegetarian Dishes: Your Guide to the Exciting World of Asian Vegetarian Cooking,* manufactured by Periplus Editions

◆ *The Ultimate Low-Fat Mexican Cookbook,* by Anne Lindsay Greer

◆ *The Lowfat Jewish Vegetarian Cookbook: Healthy Traditions from around the World,* by Debra Wasserman

◆ *Indian Regional Classics: Fast, Fresh, and Healthy Home Cooking,* by Julie Sahni

◆ *Healthy Southwestern Cooking: Less Fat, Low Salt, Lots of Flavor,* by Bob Wiseman

◆ *The Healthy Soul Food Cookbook: How to Cut the Fat but Keep the Flavor,* by Wilbert Jones

◆ *Healthy Mexican Cookbook: A Fresh Approach to Mexican Recipes,* by Jacqueline Higuera McMahan, Ruth Hightower (Editor)

◆ *Italian Cooking for a Healthy Heart: Over 140 Delicious Recipes for Low-Fat, Low-Cholesterol Gourmet Dishes,* by Joanne D'Agostino, Frank J. D'Agostino

When dining with your partner's family, be respectful of boundaries and communicate the reasons behind your eating decisions as clearly as possible. If you decline food, do so politely. Instead of saying "No thanks, I don't eat rice," try "It's delicious but no thank you," or "I couldn't have another bite. Everything is so wonderful I've overdone it," or "I'm full right now but I can't wait until next time." If you're getting pressure to eat when you don't want to, refer to the How to Fight Off a Food Pusher advice in Chapter Thirteen, page 146.

GET TO KNOW YOUR PARTNER'S FOOD CULTURE

Don't be discouraged if your partner isn't the best cultural guide. The onus may be on you to get informed and cope with family meals.

◆ *Do Your Homework.*
   Conduct library or Internet research about your partner's culture. Ask friends who share his or her background to give you the basics. Or sit down with a one or more of your partner's relatives for a lesson. Older relatives, especially, may be eager to talk about food traditions from the old country. Surprise him or her with a phrase or fact you've learned.
◆ *Plan Ahead for Holidays or Weddings.*
   Ask about what will be served and, if necessary, figure out what you can eat ahead of time.
◆ *Eat Beforehand.*
   If you don't know if you'll like the food served, have something before you go.
◆ *Be Polite about Expressing Dislike.*
   Temper rejection with acceptance. You might say, "I don't like these mushrooms, but I love the pierogies! Can I have more of those?"

By broadening his knowledge of Emily's cultural background, Brian was able to stop seeing rice just as carbs and started to see it more as an extension of her heritage. And his good manners and respect for her family's food endeared him to his future in-laws.

It'd Be So Much Easier If You'd Just Eat Meat!

HOW A VEGETARIAN AND A CARNIVORE CAN FIND A HAPPY MEDIUM

 Rachel, a twenty-two-year-old vegetarian, and Scott, a twenty-four-year-old hard-core carnivore, recently began dating. While Rachel isn't militant about other peoples' food choices, she's extremely devoted to her animal free eating habits. Scott, on the other hand, knows he could not live without meat. It's the one thing he could never give up. Initially, they tried to find restaurants that would accommodate both of their preferences. While this is fairly easy, the more time they spent together, the harder it became. Scott truly enjoys steak houses, barbecue joints, wing huts, and hot dog stands. Rachel prefers ethnic restaurants with primarily vegetarian menus, health food eateries, and salad bars.

"It would be so much easier if you weren't a vegetarian!" Scott says. When things get hectic, and they don't have time to plan ahead properly, they have a hard time finding something acceptable.

"And it's be so much easier if you were!" Rachel likes to reply.

This fight isn't really about different lifestyle choices—it's about the extra effort that goes into compromise. Scott and

Rachel will have an easier time if they discuss the reasons behind their lifestyle choices and explore more compromises.

With vegetarianism on the rise and veggie items popping up in mainstream grocery stores and restaurants across the country, there is now more acceptance of a vegetarian lifestyle than ever before. More and more health organizations are recommending a vegetarian or semi-vegetarian way of life for optimal health and disease prevention. However, talking about vegetarianism can be as controversial as discussing religion or politics. There are many misconceptions about why a person might choose not to eat meat, and discussions can easily become heated and passionate. What we eat is very personal, an important part of who we are and some people interpret a rejection of meat as a criticism or judgment of what they eat, who they are, or how they live their lives.

What Meat-Free Can Mean

THERE ARE MANY degrees of eating that minimize meat. These terms describe most of the categories.

- A **vegetarian** is someone who does not eat one or more the following: red meat, chicken, turkey, pork, fish, seafood, or any animal.
- **Ovo-lacto vegetarians** eat no meat, fish or poultry, but do consume eggs and dairy products.
- **Lacto-vegetarians** eat dairy, but not eggs.
- **Ovo-vegetarians** eat eggs, but no dairy.
- **Pesco-vegetarians** eat fish while **pollo-vegetarians** eat chicken.
- **Vegans** do not consume animal products of any kind, including meat, poultry, fish, dairy, eggs, honey, gelatin or other animal by-products or animal-derived ingredients.

HOW TO EXPLAIN YOUR WAY OF EATING

If you have recently entered into a relationship with someone who questions why you don't eat meat, keep these tips in mind.

◆ *Explain, Don't Preach*
   Before discussing your preference, make it clear that you respect your partner's choices and are not trying to convert him or her or convince them you are right and they are wrong.
◆ *Stick to the Facts*
   If you do decide to discuss your reasons for not eating meat, try to remain factual, not emotional. For helpfully worded facts and information visit Farm Sanctuary at www.vegforlife.org.

Rachel explained that her decision not to eat animals stems from health concerns related to a family history of conditions linked to the consumption of animal fat—heart disease and colon cancer. "But," she said, "I'm also motivated by my love of animals and the connection between vegetarianism and the environment. I recycle, I'm careful about conserving water and energy. I always get leaky faucets repaired immediately, and I turn the lights off when I leave the room. This is another thing I can do to make a difference."

This situation isn't exactly easy, but after they've talked about Rachael's motivations, this couple should be able to find some common ground, as long as they are both willing to give a little. *Compromise* tips include:

HOW A VEGETARIAN CAN HELP
A CARNIVORE COMPROMISE

Ask the carnivore to try some meat imitations. There are so many tasty meatless items on the market now: burgers, dogs, pepperoni, lunchmeat, meatballs, and bacon. See if the meat-eater can tell the difference, or at least note which items he or she finds acceptable. A carnivore may be willing to eat them simply because they taste good, even if he or she not planning to go veggie full-time. Or, arrange a meatless food taste test:

Faux Meat Sampler

Soy breakfast sausages and patties
Veggie burgers and dogs
Vegetarian sausages (including smoked, Italian, Bratwurst and chorizo flavored)
BBQ "beef," "ribs," and "chicken"

Prepare, cut into small pieces, place toothpicks in samples and arrange on a platter. Or make several vegetarian versions of appetizers or entrées. Tell your partner that some are vegetarian and some are not. (This is a little white lie! But it may be necessary: I've found that when someone knows going in that everything is vegetarian, they judge the products with bias. Just make sure you're partner doesn't have any wheat or soy allergies.) Ask your partner to guess which ones are vegetarian and ask him/her to rank their taste and flavor on a scale from zero to ten (ten = best). Afterwards, surprise your partner by revealing that they are all vegetarian.

There are also many meals made with meatless products that appeal to carnivores. Ask your partner to try these crowd pleasers:

Veggie Tacos

Vegetarian soy crumbles
Taco seasoning
Pico de Gallo or salsa

Shredded lettuce
Shredded cheese (or veggie cheese for vegans)
Sour cream (or non-dairy sour cream like Tofutti Sour Supreme
for vegans)
Corn tortillas

Warm crumbles in microwave according to package instructions. Add one-half to one teaspoon taco seasoning to taste. Place "meat" in the middle of warmed tortilla. Top with Pico de Gallo or salsa, lettuce, and cheese.

Pita Pizza

Oat bran or whole wheat pita
Olive oil
Pasta sauce
Veggies of choice
Vegetarian "pepperoni"
Shredded cheese (or soy cheese)

Place pita flat down on cookie sheet. Drizzle with olive oil and rub into pita. Top with pizza sauce. Add veggies. Arrange "pepperoni" onto pita and sprinkle with cheese. Heat in broiler for five to eight minutes or until cheese melts.

Veggie Hoagie

Wheat hoagie roll
Various soy lunch "meats"
(such as Yves or Lightlife brands soy turkey, salami, bologna,
Canadian bacon, etc.)
Cheese slices

(or veggie cheese such as such as Tofutti brand or Vegan
Gourmet for vegans)
Spicy mustard
Toppings: lettuce, tomato, onion, peppers, olives, oil and
vinegar, etc.

Spread hoagie with spicy mustard, arrange "meat," cheese and
toppings. Close and slice.

Meatless items are found in the produce, frozen food, or health
food sections of mainstream grocery stores. They're also available
in many health food stores and whole food markets. I've eaten
meat-free for seventeen years, and these are the Web sites I keep
coming back to for products, ingredients, and nutrition facts:

- www.bocaburger.com
- www.lightlife.com
- www.yvesveggie.com
- www.gardenburger.com
- www.morningstarfarms.com
- www.veggiepatch.com
- www.tofurkey.com
- www.nowandzen.net
- www.tofutti.com

I also cook often from these cookbooks:
- *Moosewood Restaurant Cook at Home: Fast and Easy
  Recipes for Any Day,* by the Moosewood Collective Staff
- *The Candle Cafe Cookbook: More than 150 Enlightened
  Recipes from New York's Renowned Vegan Restaurant,* by
  Joy Pierson, Bart Potenza, and Barbara Scott-Goodman
- *1,001 Low-Fat Vegetarian Recipes,* second edition, by
  Sue Spitler and Linda R. Yoakam

HOW TO MAKE MEAT
AND VEGGIE MEALS AT HOME

When cooking together at home, Rachel and Scott could use the two-versions-in-one-meal method discussed in Chapter 3. Once they both understood why they ate the way they did, it was easier for them to support each other and make compromises. You, too, can follow these easy guidelines to make your eating experiences more compatible (and enjoyable):

◆ Share veggies and starches, while cooking a soy patty and a steak on separate sides of the same grill.

◆ Add meat to one entrée at the last minute by throwing meat into pasta or the beef into stir-fry after removing a veggie portion.

◆ Bake chicken and tofu side by side in separate pans in the same oven.

◆ Make two mini pizzas, one with real pepperoni and one with veggie pepperoni.

◆ Discuss utensil use. Vegetarians usually prefer that spatulas, serving spoons and forks that come in contact with meat do not touch their food. Buy extras so you always have enough and store them in separate drawers or countertop crocks.

◆ Do take-out, twice. Order a falafel from the place around the corner from the carnivore's favorite BBQ joint. Or, order a meal and veggie sides, which the vegetarian can supplement with non-meat items from home.

◆ Make a list of the noncompatible restaurants that don't offer foods you can both enjoy. Agree to visit these restaurants with friends or coworkers or make them part of the double take-out plan.

◆ When trying a new restaurant, go online or call the restaurant to have the menu faxed to you. Previewing the menu before dining there can prevent a dining disaster.

Rachel and Scott came a long way in a few months. Instead of turning up his nose at anything vegetarian, Scott started to let taste, convenience, and energy guide his choices. Rachel's veggie burgers won him over. After he realized that they tasted good, cook in one minute, and make him feel light and energetic, he put them on the top of the shared meals list.

Rachel went from feeling like their food conflict could mean the end of their relationship to believing it was just an inconvenient difference. They dealt with it, and now the extra work is second nature.

8

Eating Healthy Is So Hard Now that We Have Kids

FAMILY FOOD THERAPY

 **Before their daughter,** Lucy, was born, Jackie, thirty-six, and George, thirty-nine, were true epicureans. They hosted dinner parties, shopped at gourmet grocery stores, and frequented new places reviewed in the local paper, or out-of-the-way places they discovered on www.chowhound.com. Jackie now works part-time, and the baby has dramatically changed her shopping and eating habits. She rarely has time to prepare distinctive dishes, and often finds herself eating "kid foods," such as dry cereal, string cheese, applesauce, and oatmeal. Jackie and George both miss the variety and freshness of the innovative foods they used to consume. Jackie sums up the situation by saying, "I can't do it all anymore. I mean, I have every intention of bringing Lucy to the market with me and preparing a healthy dinner while she naps, but something always comes up. I just can't neatly schedule blocks of time in my day planner like I used to." In addition, Jackie has not yet returned to her pre-pregnancy weight.

When a new baby joins a family, everything changes, including meals. In this case, Jackie is somewhat overwhelmed and needs a little help. In Jackie and George's case, the food conflict isn't between the two of them but between the couple and their schedules. Because hiring a nanny or assistant was not possible, my advice to Jackie is to recruit support and use outside resources. A few friends or family members may be able to pitch in, and she can set up a "trade" system with other moms and friends. Jackie said that while she has a few family members and friends in the area who'd offered to help, she didn't know how to take them up on their offers. We started by prioritizing the issues she wanted to resolve, and made the following list of her needs.

WHAT'S ON YOUR WISH LIST?

In an ideal life, we'd all have more hours in the day, less demands at work and more free time. What would you do with yours?

◆ More exercise time
◆ More time for food shopping
◆ More time for cooking
◆ More time with her partner, including date/dine out time
◆ Moving her diet away from "kid" food and toward a balanced eating plan that supports her post-pregnancy weight goal as well as her food personality

These issues are likely to be concerns for any new mom in Jackie's situation. I recommended that Jackie begin relying on friends and family to help her achieve these goals. Suggestions for each include:

HOW TO MAKE YOUR FOOD-RELATED WISHES A REALITY

WISH: *More exercise time.*

HOW TO MAKE IT HAPPEN: A mommy exchange schedule. Jackie can set up a regular schedule with another mom for watching each other's children. If Jackie watches the children each Tuesday morning and the other mom takes them each Thursday, Jackie will have at least one consistent exercise session each week.

Jackie can fit in home-based small increments of exercise. Even ten minutes here and there add up over time. Great pieces of home equipment include inflatable resistance exercise balls, stretchy bands, handheld weights, steps, and short videos. Regular short bouts of exercise will help her get back to her pre-pregnancy weight, improve her energy level, and regulate her appetite.

Shop for home equipment on:

www.reebok.com
www.sears.com
www.bodytrends.com
www.performbetter.com
www.spriproducts.com

Jogging strollers are a great way to burn extra calories while you and your little one get some fresh air. If you're not quite ready for jogging, start out walking. Listen to your body. As you increase the frequency or length of your walk and it gets easier, gradually increase your speed.

WISH: *More time for food shopping*
HOW TO MAKE IT HAPPEN: Jackie has several friends or family members without small children who offered to pick up items for her each time they shop. In exchange, Jackie offered to return the favors by baby-sitting, house-sitting, dog-sitting, and other helpful deeds, like letting the cable or phone repair service people in when they can't be home.

Shop online and use delivery services or consider hiring a personal food shopper (see pages 58–59 in Chapter Four for details).

WISH: *More time for cooking*
HOW TO MAKE IT HAPPEN: Utilize resources for quick, gourmet recipes in order to enjoy some "adult" meals without spending lots of time cooking. Web sites that offer easily accessible and often quick gourmet recipes include:

> www.foodnetwork.com
> www.epicurious.com
> www.cookinglight.com
> www.easygourmetrecipes.com

WISH: *More date/dine out time with George*
HOW TO MAKE IT HAPPEN: A regularly scheduled babysitting exchange, say the first and third Thursday of each month, allows new parents to enjoy alone time together, visit new restaurants, and reenergize. I recommend making this a pre-scheduled standing date. This can relieve Jackie of some stress by giving her a reward to look forward to. (In my work with clients, I have found that this can really help people stay on track and motivated, versus reverting back to previous problematic behaviors.)

WISH: *Achieving and maintaining dietary changes*
HOW TO MAKE IT HAPPEN: While Jackie must keep "kid" foods handy for Lucy, there is no reason she can't pack some extra "adult" snacks to enjoy herself. Some portable, healthy, grown-up items to consider are small portions of nutrient-rich dried fruit, like figs, dates, apricots, and blueberries; tofu/soy jerky, cherry or grape tomatoes, baby carrots; golf-ball sized portions of unsalted cashews, almonds, walnuts, sunflower seeds, or pecans; modest portions of whole grain crackers, pretzels, and pita bread.

Late-night heavy meals were also preventing Jackie's weight loss. Like many new parents, Jackie and George waited to eat dinner until after they put the baby to bed. Many nights, they don't finish eating until 9:30 or even 10:00 P.M. This can lead to getting overly hungry, eating too much, too fast, using the food to unwind, or eating without hunger.

HOW TO EAT LIGHT DINNERS EARLIER

When you've got small children, or even just one child like Jackie and George do, it's easy to let the evening get away from you. If you're eating late on a regular basis, assume the meal will get pushed back and strategize to eat earlier.

◆ Break up your meal. Have part of your meal before the baby's bedtime or enjoy an early evening snack so you don't overeat later.

◆ Prepare and freeze meals in advance so you can quickly reheat and eat the leftovers before it gets too late in the evening.

◆ To prevent problematic meal postponing, see the coordinating dinner tips in Chapter Four, pages 49–50.

While George works in an office, there are many things he can do and plan during the work day to help Jackie manage her time. Here are some ways he can help:

HOW TO SUPPORT A PRIMARY CAREGIVER'S FOOD-RELATED GOALS

Work on one of these goals each week:

◆ Be Predictable. Try to keep a regular work schedule so your partner can organize his or her day better.

◆ Give 'em a Night Off. Plan a regular "Daddy" or "Mommy" night and spend one evening a week or two evenings a month alone with the baby. That way, your partner can enjoy a night to his or herself; go to the bookstore, take a yoga class or a long walk, have dinner, or see a movie with a friend.

◆ Arrange Family Market Night. Grocery shop as a group so you can help watch the baby and free your partner up to focus on the food shopping without feeling rushed or distracted. Choose a night when the store is less busy to reduce extra stress or the chaos of crowded aisles and parking lots.

◆ Take over the Bath and Bedtime Routine. During the break, your partner can prepare "grown-up" meals for the week that can be frozen and re-heated.

◆ Stock up on Plastic Storage Containers. An ample supply of different shapes and sizes makes it easier to store and re-heat leftovers. Some Tupperware and Rubbermaid brand products can go right from the freezer into the microwave.

◆ Brainstorm, Plan, and Cook Meals. During the day, find dinner recipes and order the ingredients online.

◆ Hire a Sitter. This means recruiting, interviewing, and booking a qualified child-care provider.

◆ Plan a Date. Find possible restaurants, get your partner's input, and make the reservation and evening plan so all he or she has to do is show up. Just the stress of making plans can prevent primary caregivers from getting out.

◆ Find a Gym with Daycare. Your partner can squeeze in thirty minutes on an elliptical trainer while the baby plays a few feet away. Search for a club near you on these sites:

    www.acefitness.org/clublocator/index.cfm
    www.healthclubs.com
    www.healthclubdirectory.com

Jackie was so overwhelmed that she didn't quite know where to begin. After reviewing these options, she and George had developed a plan. With help from George, her family and friends,

Fresh Direct, and epicurious.com, Jackie started working out regularly at a gym with child-care, got a handle on grocery shopping and cooking by ordering online, and even managed to sneak out a couple nights a month for dinners. George and Jackie adjusted to their first baby but what if they have another?

After Pia, forty-four, and Jimmy, forty-five, had their second child, Pia decided to stay home full-time. The kids, Cameron and Alex, now four and seven, really know what foods they like and dislike, and that can make family meals difficult. Even with all her time at home, Pia can't find foods that everyone enjoys. "What am I supposed to do?" she asked me. "I can't cook four different meals to please everyone in my family!"

I hear this complaint all the time. Couples with more than one child face even more challenges than parents of one. As children grow, their food personalities grow too. Between the ages of four and eight[1], kids develop very strong food personalities. Any parent of more than one child knows that their likes and dislikes can be worlds apart. Luckily, there are ways to find meals everyone enjoys. The secret is to get the kids involved in meal planning and preparation. This way it's less likely that they will flat out reject what's served.

Parents in this predicament can reduce stress by applying the negotiation and imagination parts of the SANITY model. Managing expectations and turning food preparation into a fun activity that the kids are a part of—instead of subjected to—can quell mealtime mania.

[1] Skinner, et al. "Children's Food Preferences: A Longitudinal Analysis." *Journal of the American Dietetic Association,* 102, no. 11 (2002): 1638–1647.

HOW TO FIND MEALS
THE WHOLE FAMILY ENJOYS

Before you can change kids' diets, you'll have to change your—and their—attitudes.

♦ Don't Stress if They Don't Eat. It's not a big deal if your kid won't eat or insists on eating the same thing over and over. These habits are more problematic for parents than for kids. Kids instinctively eat the amount that their bodies need. Stay calm, and eventually your child will eat, or try something new. You can encourage them to eat other by offering a selection along with their daily peanut-butter-and-jelly sandwich.

♦ Get Everyone Involved. If the kids share the food shopping and preparation responsibilities, they'll take the pressure off mom and dad. And learning more about food—where it comes from (before getting to the grocery store), what it looks like before it's prepared, and how to prepare it can help kids sharpen their geography, math, and science skills and develop a broader food personality. Kids are inquisitive by nature. Sparking an interest in food can also help them develop a healthier relationship with food so they see it as more than just a reward or habit.

♦ Try Kid-Friendly Starters. Let the little ones start out eating healthy snacks while you prepare the main course. And don't feel bad if you park them in front of the TV for thirty minutes during prep time. Some kid-friendly starter suggestions: one hundred percent applesauce, baby carrots (softened in microwave), mashed banana, yogurt, one hundred percent fruit juice, string or grated or cottage cheese, low-fiber, low-sugar dry cereal (like Cherrios), pre-cooked macaroni with a tiny bit of tomato sauce, Cream of Wheat.

◆ Use a Sitter while You're Home. Having someone to watch your kids while you prepare meals can make mealtime much less hectic. Or, invite a friend or relative over for a casual dinner with the understanding that they'll keep an eye on the little ones while you prep and cook.

◆ Teach Them about Food and Nutrition. Check out these children's books from the local library to help kids get informed and interested. A few good picks:

➤ *Good Enough to Eat: A Kid's Guide to Food and Nutrition,* by Lizzy Rockwell

➤ *The Edible Pyramid: Good Eating Every Day,* by Loreen Leedy

➤ *Nutrition for Every Kid: Easy Activities That Make Learning Science Fun,* by Janice VanCleave

➤ *Eat Up! Healthy Food for a Healthy Earth,* by Candace C. Savage, Gary Clement (Illustrator)

➤ *Cows are Vegetarians: A Book for Vegetarian Kids,* by Ann Bradley, Elise Huffman (Illustrator), and Stephen Kramer (Illustrator)

◆ Appoint the Kids as Grocery Shopping Assistants. Ask the kids to help create a grocery list. Give them "jobs" to do at the store, like reading the aisle signs to locate items, checking items off the list, organizing and unloading the cart at checkout, packing the groceries, keeping track of how much money is spent, and so on.

◆ Put Them to Work. Have older kids help with the entire meal, including washing and peeling vegetables, setting the table, clearing and washing dishes, and properly storing leftovers. Teens can help by searching for new recipes on the Internet, chopping vegetables, and loading the dishwasher. Don't limit prep work to just the girls in the family. Teaching boys to prepare food helps prepare them for healthy eating as adults.

- ◆ Call a Family Food Meeting. Get together to discuss and plan the week's menus. Then use the weekly menus to create a grocery list.
- ◆ Book 'em: Help your child connect recipes to real food by experimenting with simple, kid-friendly cookbooks. The fun illustrations and graphics help little ones understand that spending time in the kitchen isn't just for grown-ups. Some of my favorite cookbooks for kids are:
  - ➤ *Children's Quick and Easy Cookbook,* by Angela Wilkes (Hardcover)
  - ➤ *Emeril's There's a Chef in My Soup!: Recipes for the Kid in Everyone,* by Emeril Lagasse and Charles Yuen (Illustrator)
  - ➤ *The Mix-It-Up Cookbook: Make More than 100 Dishes from 18 Basic Recipes,* by American Girl Library, Tracy McGuiness (Illustrator)
  - ➤ *Kids' First Cookbook: Delicious-Nutritious Treats To Make Yourself!,* by the American Cancer Society
  - ➤ *Betty Crocker Kids Cook!,* by Betty Crocker Editors

It took several months, but after Cameron and Alex got into the swing of dinner starter snacks, as well a little food planning and preparation, the family food tensions eased up. On a good day, Cameron tries a new vegetable (as long as there's some parmesan cheese sprinkled on top) and Alex, as well as his parents, have become slightly more flexible about food. Once Pia got them into a routine of eating a starter snack while they watched a video or played a CD, she was able to approach dinner more sanely and calmly. That relaxed meal made the rest of the evening more manageable, and by getting the kids started on the dinner earlier, she got the meal on the table sooner, and got them into bed at a much more reasonable hour.

Stop Feeding Him Scraps!

HOW PET FEEDING REFLECTS BIGGER FOOD ATTITUDES

 **Christine, twenty-sevn, and Eric,** twenty-eight, are the proud parents of two cats and a dog and have contradictory care-giving styles. Eric feeds their yellow lab, Lucky, table scraps and sneaks the cats treats. Eric loves watching Lucky lick his chops and then say thank you by placing his furry head on "daddy's" feet. Otto, their orange tabby, repays the favor by curling up on Eric's lap while he surfs the web. While Christine wants to spoil the pets as well, she sees the extra indulgences as unnecessary and unhealthy. All three animals are overweight and she worries about their health risks. She has asked Eric to cut back, and he will, temporarily, but he gives in eventually.

"Look at his eyes," he'll say, "How can I resist? Otto and Pepper are crying for their treats!"

Although Christine and Eric's own eating habits are in sync, their opposing feeding attitudes toward the pets have created a great deal of conflict in their relationship.

I met Christine and Eric at a dinner party. When they found out what I do for a living they jokingly asked if I take clients of the feline and canine persuasions. "Yeah, we're okay, but our pets have serious eating disorders," Eric said.

Pulling away from Eric and sitting up straight, Christine said, irritably, "Well, if Eric wouldn't keep feeding them junk *all* the time they wouldn't expect it."

"Christine," Eric chided, defensively, "you're just way too strict." There were serious emotions brewing here. When I told them that while I've never had a couple schedule an appointment specifically about pet issues, they do come up in nutrition counseling. Your pets are a reflection of you and an extension of your family. Some pet owners treat their pets better than they treat themselves: they purchase premium pet food but eat junk food themselves. Some take their pets to the vet for regular check-ups and vaccinations but avoid their own personal medical care. In other cases, a pet owner's own dysfunctional relationship with food is extended to Fluffy or Fido: they feed themselves and their pets when they're bored, upset, or sad. And sometimes, pets become the pawns in their owners' emotional troubles. Your partner may compete—consciously or unconsciously—for a pup's attention by showering him or her with treats. Most significantly, relationship conflicts about how to feed pets can foreshadow future quarrels about how to feed children. Working through seemingly trivial pet feeding issues can help you resolve unhealthy habits of your own, improve your pet's health, and prepare you both for making mutual nutritional decisions should you have kids.

Our dogs and cats serve such important roles in our lives. They love us unconditionally, make us laugh and feel happy, and reach out to us when they sense that we're really needy. "After I've had a long day, just seeing my cat run to the door when I get home can melt my tension," I told Christine and Eric. "When I'm sad, he snuggles up to me, rubbing his head on my cheek to comfort me, even licking my tears away. I hate it when I'm traveling and he sleeps on my husband's pillow instead of mine."

After they realized they weren't alone in their dilemma, Christine and Eric began to open up and talk freely.

"Christine works closer to home so she gets to walk Lucky every day during the week. I miss that so I guess I bond with him through food," Eric said.

Christine turned to Eric with a surprised look on her face. "Really?" she asked, "I didn't know you felt that way."

"Neither did I until I just said it," Eric replied.

This kind of *honesty* and communication was just what the couple needed. Their ongoing arguments had been about behaviors—what, how much, and when to feed the pets—but they hadn't discussed the frank reasons for their actions.

We are a society of producers and caretakers. Working hard and living up to responsibilities are rewarded. Particularly for women, putting others' needs before our own is the norm. Many of my clients feel selfish taking care of themselves, because it's simply not encouraged in this day and age. Getting enough sleep, eating well, exercising, getting a massage, even reading for pleasure seem like luxuries.

Indulging ourselves with food, however, is an acceptable, accessible, and simple way to do something nice for ourselves. When we begin this habit, it "works" in the respect that it feels good in the moment. When we adopt food as a substitute for other caretaking behaviors, however, we may pass this behavior onto our pets or allow them to become our partners in crime. It's yet another activity we can share with them and pets can't "tell" on us. We know our secret is safe.

"I hear that," Eric offered. "If I've had a really bad day, sometimes all I want to do is veg out in front of the TV with a beer, a bag of Cheetos, and Lucky. He loves Cheetos. He catches them in his mouth. I mean, it's fun but Christine gets so bent out of shape."

This may be part of the reason why pets, like people, are growing more and more overweight and running a higher risk of health problems like heart disease and diabetes.

═══════════════════

How to Know if Your Pet Is Overweight

YOU SHOULD BE able to tell if your furry friend is too heavy just by looking at 'em.

DOGS ARE OVERWEIGHT IF . . .
- ◆ You can't feel the animal's ribs.
- ◆ He or she has fat deposits on the back or tail base.
- ◆ It's hard to see the pet's waist.

CATS ARE OVERWEIGHT IF . . .
- ◆ The abdomen is rounded.
- ◆ He or she has fat deposits on his face, back, or limbs
- ◆ The cat simply looks fat[2].

═══════════════════

Pets, like humans, respond to learned behaviors and develop habits. Every pet owner swears their dog or cat is the smartest animal on Earth because they know the sound of the can opener or the refrigerator opening. The truth is, they do! Once you've started a habit of rewarding your pet with food, your pet may come to expect this, and when you don't deliver the goods you may feel like you're letting Fluffy or Fido down. Because we love our pets and are so emotionally bonded with them, we don't like disappointing them. Pets truly are our best friends. So, seeing your pet bond more with your partner than with you can cause you to compete for their affection, using food as leverage for attention.

After taking an honest look at their individual and joint relationship with their pets, Christine and Eric were ready to negotiate and *compromise*. They needed to focus on what they have in

[2] National Academies' National Research Council Revised Nutrient Requirement of Dogs and Cats, 2003

common—their love for their animals. Christine explained that when the pets beg, she wants to give in just as much as he does, but she has made the connection between their nutrition and their health. In the moment, she thinks about how not giving in means taking better care of them and recalls the articles she's read online. "I know being overweight is bad for Lucky's joints," she says, "and I don't want the kitties to end up with diabetes. I see how my co-worker Maria has to give her cat insulin shots and it just breaks my heart." Keeping that information in the front of her mind helps to raise her awareness about what choice to make in the moment.

Ask the Vet

IF YOU'RE HAVING a hard time limiting your pet's diet, talk to the vet. He or she can explain why overweight dogs and cats are at greater risk for dangerous health problems. Ask specific questions, like these:

- How would my pet's health improve if he or she lost weight?
- What are the potential consequences if he or she doesn't lose weight?
- How much should we cut back?
- What kind of results can we expect in what time frame?

Eric needs to be on board with this association before he'll be willing to change his behavior. He has to believe that the rewards of not giving in are greater than what he and his pets are giving up. I suggested the couple *reach out* to outside help and schedule a *joint* meeting with their veterinarian. Sometimes one "parent" is in charge of a pet's medical care and gains a better understanding of the animal's health needs. This can disconnect the other partner from understanding the dangers of obesity and the importance of limiting food. At a joint meeting, the vet can objectively confirm that overweight dogs and cats are at greater risk for health problems and explain why.

Also, talking to the vet might help Eric say no to the furry friends who count on him to do the right thing for their health. If an immediate meeting isn't practical, the following pet health Web sites can help educate owners about nutrition:

Pet Health Resources

WHILE THE INTERNET is packed with pet feeding information, much of it is unreliable or advertises specific pet foods. Check out these trustworthy sites:

www.avma.org/care4pets

www.vet.cornell.edu

www.healthypet.com

www.nlm.nih.gov/medlineplus/petsandpethealth.html

Eric must also find alternative ways to bond with the pets that does not involve food. Early morning walks with Lucky, one-on-one play time with each animal, or extra alone time with them on the weekends might do the trick.

Next, Christine and Eric can develop a firm plan for feeding the pets, agreeing on the type of food, amount, and timing. In addition, they can gather ideas from their vet about increasing the amount of exercise their pets receive. Finally, they can discuss a strategy for keeping each other on track, such as a phrase or motto.

My husband and I have faced this situation ourselves. After

imposing a new healthy feeding routine, we were awakened at 2:00 A.M. to find our cats chowing down on a pile of "put away" food they knocked off a high shelf in the laundry room. As we were cleaning the last of it, my husband said, "The buffet is now closed." This sentence has become our motto for helping to keep each other on target with our goals for our pets—but it also comes in handy when we need to support our own healthy habits.

I suggested that Christine and Eric find one of their own, and suggested phrases like these:

◆ That's all folks.
◆ Show's over.
◆ Nothing more to see here, move along.

Finally, I encouraged Eric and Christine to find non-food ways of pampering their pets. They asked other animal-loving friends for advice and created this list:

WAYS TO PAMPER YOUR PETS

Cats

◆ Grooming with a special cat brush or comb.
◆ Give them fun, cat-specific toys, such as feathers, balls, and catnip-filled stuffed animals.
◆ Some cats love watching videos. Try *The Purrfect Video* from TV Time Productions, available at retail and book stores.

Dogs

◆ Take your dog to a campground that accepts canines.
◆ Take your dog for a ride in the car with the windows down.

- Visit the dog run or dog park.
- Take your dog for a visit to Petsmart or another pet-friendly store where you can pick up a toy.
- Give your dog a doggie playdate.

Cats or Dogs

- Play with them daily, even if it's just for ten minutes.
- Give them cushy bedding that's just for them.

After six months of fewer food treats, Lucky, Otto, and Pepper had all slimmed down and were noticeably more energetic, playful, and happy. Their successful dietary change even inspired Christine and Eric to become more active. Now their weekend routine includes an early morning jog in the park with Lucky.

10

I'm Too Hungry to Be Nice!

FOOD AND MOOD SWINGS

Jeremy, twenty-six, had been dating Chloe, twenty-five, for six months before she revealed her ugly side. They'd just found a new apartment and set out to furnish and decorate it. After a quick cup of coffee, they embarked on a shopping extravaganza. They hit Target, Crate & Barrel, and then moved on to Pottery Barn and Bed, Bath & Beyond. Six hours into their spree, Chloe's playful persona turned short-tempered and sarcastic. "Why do you always pick red, I hate red!" she'd snap. Or, "Forget it, the line's too long," and, "Just make up your mind already." Jeremy had never seen Chloe act so mean and it freaked him out.

Jeremy, a long-term client I helped get in shape to pass his firefighter's exam, called shortly after this spat. He wondered if Chloe's irregular eating schedule had something do with her mood swings. "I remember how moody and tired I was when I wasn't getting enough fat and carbs," he said. "Do you think this is something like that?"

I wasn't familiar with Chloe's eating pattern, medical history, or recent lifestyle changes so I really couldn't say. But since irregular eating is such a common problem in our rushed world, I had a hunch Jeremy was right. Many busy people skip meals and don't eat until their blood sugar levels have already plummeted and made them irritable. I emailed Jeremy a general food mood record (illustrated below) and a hunger/fullness graph (See Chapter Four, pages 47–48.). I suggested Jeremy ask Chloe to fill out the Mood Record (illustrated below) for three days, including one weekend day. You can complete this chart, too.

Jeremy might approach Chloe about completing the chart by saying something like this: "I have some nutrition worksheets I used when I was training. I thought you'd like to try them because with all the changes going on lately I know it's been crazy and they really helped me."

I've found that irregular eaters who suffer from irritability usually know there's a problem and are open to help. As long as you don't approach them while their blood sugar is crashing, they cooperate.

The following week, Jeremy called for a quick consult to review Chloe's results.

Chloe's Food Mood Record

MEAL (i.e., breakfast snack, lunch...)	FOOD/BEVERAGES CONSUMED	TIME	PLACE	MOOD PRIOR TO MEAL	MOOD AFTER MEAL

Chloe's Food Mood Record

MEAL (i.e., breakfast snack, lunch…)	FOOD/BEVERAGES CONSUMED	TIME	PLACE	MOOD PRIOR TO MEAL	MOOD AFTER MEAL
Snack	Latte	9:00 A.M.	Starbucks	Neutral	Neutral
Snack	Popcorn, diet Coke	12:30 P.M.	Target	Cranky, tired	Cranky, tired
Dinner	Garden salad, black bean soup, iced tea, oatmeal cookie	7:00 P.M.	Panera Bread	Irritable, emotional	Neutral
Snack	Grapes	10:30 P.M.	Home	Tired	Neutral

Her paperwork didn't surprise me. Chloe's eating pattern was no pattern at all. The timing, quantity, and quality of her meals varied dramatically from day to day. Whenever she went more than four hours without food, she felt cranky, easily irritated, and overly emotional. Soon after she ate, her energy level and mood returned to normal. However, the long gaps between meals often resulted in overeating, which sometimes caused Chloe to eat too much and get too full. When this happened, Chloe's mood and blood sugar swung from one end of the pendulum to the other. She'd get hungry and cranky, wolf down a big meal, and then feel bloated and lethargic.

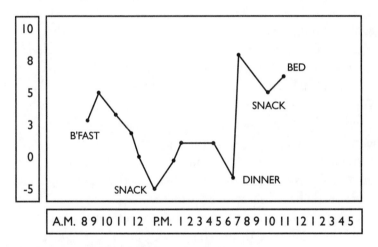

−5 = out of control hunger (shaky, trouble concentrating)
 0 = comfortably hungry (non-intense feeling of emptiness but no discomfort)
 3 = physically full but not satisfied (still thinking about food)
 5 = full (but not overly full), satsified and energized
 8 = uncomfortably full (feelings of pressure, slight discomfort, sluggish)
10 = painfully full (intense pressure or pain, need to lay down, take antacids, change into looser clothing, very sluggish)

Aim to stay in the middle of the scale. Eat at a 0 (when comfortably hungry) and stop at 5 (when you're feeling comfortably full, satisfied and energized).

After we reviewed the results, I pointed out the connections between Chloe's meal timing and her moods. Chloe became withdrawn. Jeremy turned to her and said, "It's true. Every time we spend the day running errands or doing some other long project you run out of energy."

Blushing and clearly uncomfortable, Chloe responded slowly. "I was so routined before we met. I ate at exactly the same time every day and always had the same weekend routine. I'm just not used to being off that kind of schedule. I'm not saying I'm not happy. I guess I'm just adjusting," she said.

Chloe's reaction to a change in routine is quite normal. I explained that once a pattern is established, the body becomes accustomed to it. Our bodies get used to the timing and duration of our sleep, the frequency, intensity, and duration of our fitness routines, and the timing, quantity, and quality of our meals. As we adapt to a well-established pattern, our bodies expect it and regulate energy levels, metabolism, and mood to it. When that pattern is disrupted, the system goes awry. The body no longer knows what to expect. Our blood sugar, strength, endurance, and mood go off-kilter.

It's similar to starting a new exercise routine. In the beginning, your muscles are sore because they aren't used to the stress. Your heart rate increases easily and you get out of breath with little exertion. With repeated sessions, however, the workout gets easier and easier. Your muscles, heart, and lungs adapt and, before you know it, the formerly tiring exercise is a piece of cake. If you stop working out regularly and you get out of shape, you quickly lose the strength and energy you gained, and have to start back at square one.

Eating is the same way. In today's on-the-go culture, it may be difficult to be a perfect eater and have healthy and balanced meals all the time. But you don't need to, as long as you maintain a steady intake of calories and nutrients in the form of snacks and beverages.

Once Chloe realized that her reactions were normal, her body language softened and she was eager to hear more. Chloe's "food prescription" was to maintain regular timing of her eating, regardless of what she ate. After discussing her symptoms, Chloe decided that the four-hour mark was where she began to lose steam. Her initial goal: never let more than four-hours pass without eating. She would strive for eating every three and a half hours, even if it meant setting the alarm on her cell phone or watch as a reminder.

Can't Remember to Eat Every Four Hours?

TRY SETTING A watch or cell phone alarm as a reminder or ask your partner to give you a heads-up.

There are lots of ways eaters with a tendency to get cranky can keep their moods level, especially if they have their partner's support and understanding.

HOW TO PREVENT HUNGER-RELATED MOOD SWINGS

Small snacks and small steps will help you minimize crankiness.

- ◆ Keep a food mood journal and a hunger fullness graph every day until your symptoms are under control. These worksheets will give you the best information about how to manage the timing, quantity, and quality of meals and snacks.
- ◆ Keep readily available snacks on hand as emergency backups (see Eating in Sync Healthy Snacks in Chapter Four, pages 50–51).
- ◆ Work with your partner to plan ahead. Before embarking on your day, think about when and where

you'll stop for a meal or snack. If you're unsure where
you'll be able to stop for a bite, pack your own snack.

◆ Ask your partner to recognize regular meals and snacks
as an important health and relationship priority. When
your body is well taken care of, you will feel better, and
relate to him or her better. Regular eating may ease
unnecessary tension.

◆ Ask your partner to help identify your symptoms. In
addition to being short-tempered, people who need food
can experience skin tone change, shaky hands, loss of
breath, difficulty concentrating, slowed speech, perspira-
tion, and headaches. If your partner notices a sudden
shift in your behavior or appearance, he or she can think
back to when you last ate and ask if you need a break or
a snack. My husband has learned to recognize the difference between my foul moods and my hunger. When I'm
in a bad mood I get wide-eyed, quiet, and withdrawn.
But when I'm hungry, watch out, I have a comment for
everything and I tend to frown. When he recognizes the
signs he'll ask, "Do you need to eat a Luna bar or something?" His ability to see when I'm crashing has saved us
from unnecessary arguments. Now I always carry a bar
or other snack in my bag as a back up.

◆ Plan ahead. When your partner picks you up to run an
errand before heading home for a meal, ask him or her
to bring a healthy tide-over snack to help keep moods
level. Some healthy options include:

> fruit, such as a small banana, an apple, washed
grapes in a baggie or sealed container

> animal crackers, pretzels, dry cereal, or whole grain
crackers

> a low-calorie energy bar, such as Pria or Luna (under
two hundred calories each)

> a tiny package of peanuts, almonds, or cashews

> a bottle or box of fruit juice

➤ a latte made with skim or soy milk
➤ a yogurt

◆ Stash non-perishable snacks like health bars or pretzel bags in the glove compartment of your car. Carry a small Tupperware container or baggie filled with nuts.

◆ Stock up on fruit juice boxes and bottles, health bars, and Ziplock bags at warehouse stores like Costco or Sam's Club.

◆ Work with your partner to plan ahead. If you have a long day, plot out when and where you'll stop to eat instead of just pushing through without eating.

◆ Remind your partner to eat. If you know he or she is having a long day at work, call and offer a gentle reminder.

Relieved and well-prepared for their big move and the work to follow, Chloe and Jeremy felt confident about their ability to prevent the hunger monster from rearing its ugly head again. They started their relationship off on the right foot by making Chloe's health a priority. Now that they are more in tune with each other's mood, they can easily recognize when the other is off balance.

Once Chloe gets used to snacking every three and a half to four hours, she can graduate to healthier snacks. The following quiz helps people determine which nutritious snacks appeal to their tastes and moods.

WHAT AM I IN THE MOOD FOR?

If you nibble on something that fills you up but just doesn't "do it" for you, you may continue thinking about food and even continue eating. That can lead to feeling sluggish, getting uncomfortably full, and gaining weight. When you're hungry, use this quiz to figure out what will really hit the spot—what will satisfy you so you can enjoy your snack and prevent overeating.

Choose one response from each of the following four questions:

1. Which texture do I want?
a) Crunchy
b) Creamy
c) Chewy
d) Watery

2. Which temperature?
a) Hot/warm
b) Cold/frozen
c) Room temperature/neutral

3. Which flavor?
a) Salty
b) Sweet
c) Sour
d) Savory
e) Bitter

4. Which taste?
a) Spicy
b) Mild

After circling your responses, write each of them down and use your food personality to make a list of two to five snacks that meet your craving criteria. Choose the one that appeals most to you.

Here are some examples:

I want something crunchy, cold, sweet, and mild.

Healthy crunchy, cold, sweet, and mild snacks include:

◆ Frozen bananas
◆ Frozen grapes

- Juice pops
- Apple wedges dipped in chilled peanut butter
- Frozen dark chocolate chips
- Unsalted peanuts and dark chocolate chips

Healthy creamy, warm, sweet, and spicy snacks include:

- Cinnamon oatmeal
- Warm applesauce with spices
- Warm rice pudding
- Chai tea w/skim or soy milk
- Flavored decaf or regular coffee with skim milk
- Sugar free, skim milk hot chocolate

Healthy crunchy, room temperature, salty, and spicy snacks include:

- Mesquite flavored pretzels
- Spicy nuts
- Chips and salsa
- Popcorn sprinkled with Cajun spices
- Sunflower seeds

Healthy creamy, cold, sweet, and mild snacks include:

- Yogurt
- Pudding
- Frozen yogurt
- Fruit juice

11

Look What
I Made for You!

FOOD AS LOVE ISSUES

Sarah, twenty-nine, recently moved into Conrad's, thirty, apartment. Eight months and eight pounds later, she's feeling fat. Her clothes are uncomfortably snug, especially her jeans. Approaching her thirtieth birthday, she is more body conscious than ever.

She believes her weight gain is related to her new boyfriend. A great cook and baker, Conrad always makes her fabulous dinners. As she he gets to know him better, Sarah suspects this has something to do with Conrad's family. His German parents and grandparents showed love with food and frequently made marzipan, candied ginger, Germknodel (dumplings), and Mohr Im Hemd (chocolate hazelnut pudding). He was very well cared for and very well fed.

Early on, Conrad expressed his love for Sarah by cooking her breakfast, planning a candlelit dinner, or surprising her with chocolates. Now, he presents a different treat nearly every week. When Sarah came home last week, Conrad had prepared a platter of breads and fruit to dip into bubbly pots of cheese and chocolate fondue. Sarah often wakes up on Sunday mornings to find him whipping up cheese blintzes and praline crepes.

Sarah knows how much Conrad delights in feeding her. And while she truly appreciates his generosity (and the fact that she snagged a man who can cook!), she has mixed feelings about the delicious foods that are making her plump.

Sarah's story is familiar. Many Americans use food to deal with emotions or to express feelings. We celebrate with food on birthdays and holidays and even bring food to those who are grieving. We take care of family by feeding each other and bond by sharing meals.

I asked Sarah if she he had discussed her weight gain with Conrad. She said Conrad shrugged off her comments, saying, "We all gain a little weight closer to thirty. Besides, you could use a little meat on your bones."

"I'm afraid I'll keep gaining weight if we don't talk about this," she said. "but I can't figure out how to do it without hurting his feelings."

Sarah scheduled a consultation to address her recent weight gain, and asked Conrad to come along.

At the meeting, Sarah repeated her concerns about those extra eight pounds, and her desire to achieve and maintain a healthy body as she ages. "I asked Conrad to come today," Sarah explained, "because he is our fabulous cook."

It's very helpful for couples to come in together when one partner prepares the meals. I asked Sarah to review her usual eating and physical activity patterns with me while Conrad quietly observed. Sarah's semi-vegetarian diet was fairly balanced: three meals and one or two well-timed snacks each day. She regularly gets her five fruits and vegetables and she works out three to five times a week.

"Have you made any changes to your diet or exercise program recently?" I asked.

"Well," she started hesitantly, "I have been eating more that I used to." Sarah looked at Conrad and continued, "We both love good food. I used to allow myself a really good dessert or rich meal occasionally, but lately we've been indulging every week, sometimes more."

"Ahh," I said. "That could certainly account for your recent weight gain." The amount Sarah used to eat was right on track with what she needed to support her "ideal" weight, the stable weight she had maintained until now.

When we take in more calories than our bodies can use, the excess calories are stored in our fat cells. Indulging in an occasional, even monthly treat isn't enough of an excess to produce weight gain in an active healthy adult. In fact, most people naturally compensate by increasing their activity level to maintain a stable body composition. But when the excesses occur regularly, and physical activity isn't increased to compensate, surplus calories add up to surplus pounds.

Sarah had three options. She could:

1. Increase physical activity by one to two hours per week to burn off the extra calories.
2. Budget calories, carbs, and fat grams within meals so she can indulge at night. For example, have a low-carb, low-fat entrée like a grilled tofu salad to make room for a high-carb, high-fat dessert like tiramisu.
3. Cut out the excess treats and go back to indulging once a month.

Sarah was silent, thinking. "Since you two eat together," I said to Conrad, "how do you feel about Sarah changing her eating habits?"

"Well, personally I think Sarah looks beautiful at the weight she's at," he replied. "And we really enjoy good food so I'm not sure it's realistic to give that up."

"Conrad, I love it when you surprise me with breakfast or chocolates but you know I'm uncomfortable with my weight," Sarah said. "My clothes are getting tighter, I don't feel like myself, I don't like putting on a bathing suit or shorts. You heard what she said, I have to cut back. I don't have time to work out more."

"But you love good food—"

"I know, but it's not the only thing I love."

Conrad sat quietly with his arms crossed. He wasn't quite on board with changing their routine. Sarah was flustered.

When entering into a relationship, each partner brings his or her unique food personality as well as his or her personal "relationship" with food. Food personalities and relationships with food are much deeper than which foods you like. Your relationship with food is the role food plays in your life, and that changes all the time.

Many times when we're under stress, we use food for emotional reasons and the food itself takes on a different purpose in our lives. Instead of sustaining our physical existence, we use it to fill a void, distract us from our problems, or comfort us. When this happens, our relationship with food becomes dysfunctional because eating is being used as a coping mechanism. This may cause problems in our personal lives or romantic relationships because we have not found a healthy way to deal.

This tool helps explain relationships with food. Using this quiz, couples will see how their relationships with food differ from one another and how those differences impact day-to-day eating habits.

WHAT'S YOUR RELATIONSHIP TO FOOD?

1. I enjoy food/eating.
a) Yes
b) No
c) Not sure

2. Food played an important role in my family.
a) Yes
b) No
c) Not sure

3. Please circle all that apply. In my family, food was used:
   a) For nourishment
   b) For enjoyment/gratification (regardless of hunger)
   c) As a recreational activity (something to do)
   d) To celebrate
   e) To comfort
   f) To show love/affection/to bond
   g) As punishment
   h) Other (please list)
   i) None of the above

4. Please circle all that apply. I believe I use food:
   a) For nourishment
   b) For enjoyment/gratification (regardless of hunger)
   c) As a recreational activity (something to do)
   d) To celebrate
   e) To comfort myself
   f) To relax
   g) When I am bored
   h) When I am angry
   i) To punish myself
   j) Other (please list)

5. Just before I eat, I am aware if I'm hungry or not.
   a) All of the time
   b) Most of the time
   c) Some of the time
   d) Rarely
   e) Never

6. Food is an important part of my social life.
   a) Yes
   b) No
   c) Not sure

7. Food is an important part of my relationship with my partner.
a) Yes
b) No
c) Not sure

8. I use food to express my love/affection for others or to bond with people.
a) Often
b) Sometimes
c) Rarely
d) Never

9. I feel disappointed/let down if others do not share my enthusiasm for food.
a) Yes
b) No
c) Not sure

10. I feel that food takes up too much of my time and energy.
a) Yes
b) No
c) Not sure

Sarah and Conrad agreed to take the quiz. Here are their responses:

Sarah's Responses:

1. I enjoy food/eating.
a. Yes
b. No
c. Not sure

2. Food played an important role in my family.
   a. Yes
   b. No
   c. Not sure

3. Please circle all that apply. In my family, food was used:
   a. For nourishment
   b. For enjoyment/gratification (regardless of hunger)
   c. As a recreational activity (something to do)
   d. To celebrate
   e. To comfort
   f. To show love/affection/to bond
   g. As punishment
   h. Other (please list)
   i. None of the above

4. Please circle all that apply. I believe I use food:
   a. For nourishment
   b. For enjoyment/gratification (regardless of hunger)
   c. As a recreational activity (something to do)
   d. To celebrate
   e. To comfort myself
   f. To relax
   g. When I am bored
   h. When I am angry
   i. To punish myself
   j. Other (please list)

5. Just before I eat, I am aware of if I'm hungry or not.
   a. All of the time
   b. Most of the time
   c. Some of the time
   d. Rarely
   e. Never

6. Food is an important part of my social life.
   a. Yes
   b. No
   c. Not sure

7. Food is an important part of my relationship with my partner.
   a. Yes
   b. No
   c. Not sure

8. I use food to express my love/affection for others or to bond with people.
   a. Often
   b. Sometimes
   c. Rarely
   d. Never

9. I feel disappointed/let down if others do not share my enthusiasm for food.
   a. Yes
   b. No
   c. Not sure

10. I feel that food takes up too much of my time and energy.
   a. Yes
   b. No
   c. Not sure

Conrad's responses:

1. I enjoy food/eating.
   a. Yes
   b. No
   c. Not sure

2. Food played an important role in my family.
   a. Yes
   b. No
   c. Not sure

3. Please circle all that apply. In my family, food was used:
   a. For nourishment
   b. For enjoyment/gratification (regardless of hunger)
   c. As a recreational activity (something to do)
   d. To celebrate
   e. To comfort
   f. To show love/affection/to bond
   g. As punishment
   h. Other (please list) Other emotions (I'm sorry...)
   i. None of the above

4. Please circle all that apply. I believe I use food:
   a. For nourishment
   b. For enjoyment/gratification (regardless of hunger)
   c. As a recreational activity (something to do)
   d. To celebrate
   e. To comfort myself
   f. To relax
   g. When I am bored
   h. When I am angry
   i. To punish myself
   j. Other (please list)

5. Just before I eat, I am aware if I'm hungry or not.
   a. All of the time
   b. Most of the time
   c. Some of the time
   d. Rarely
   e. Never

6. Food is an important part of my social life.
   a. Yes
   b. No
   c. Not sure

7. Food is an important part of my relationship with my partner.
   a. Yes
   b. No
   c. Not sure

8. I use food to express my love/affection for others or to bond with people.
   a. Often
   b. Sometimes
   c. Rarely
   d. Never

9. I feel disappointed/let down if others do not share my enthusiasm for food.
   a. Yes
   b. No
   c. Not sure

10. I feel that food takes up too much of my time and energy.
   a. Yes
   b. No
   c. Not sure

After comparing each other's answers, Conrad said, "I can't believe a little quiz can open my eyes this much. I know that Sarah and I have very different answers."

Conrad recalled childhood episodes when his mother and grandmother gave him food when he really wanted a hug. He was the youngest child of a mother who, as a musician, traveled often. Whenever she came back from a trip, she brought him a special treat: chocolate truffles, peanut brittle, and almond macaroons. She always told Conrad he was her special sweetie and said, "Sweets for my sweetie."

"I adored my mother and grandmother," he said, "but they never verbally expressed their feelings. When I came home from college for the holidays, they prepared a feast and greeted me at the door with an armful of strudel! Food has always been the way my family takes care of each other. I can see now that I do that with Sarah." He frowned at Sarah, who responded with a tender smile. Sarah had already realized this.

By opening up and starting to come to terms with their relationships with food, Conrad and Sarah achieved *honesty*. They never could have gotten this far without Sarah's frankness about her weight gain, and both of their willingness to analyze themselves with the quiz. Now that they understand their food conflict, their imaginations can help them find creative new ways to move forward.

Outside help is also crucial here and involves expanding the support network. I referred Conrad to a psychotherapist who does a lot of work looking at how childhood family dynamics impact adult relationships. Conrad just scratched the surface of some family issues and a psychotherapist could really help him delve further into them. Therapy could have a tremendously positive impact on Conrad and Sarah's relationship and help with the food issues we touched on.

Sarah is thrilled about the changes they've made. She started losing weight and she and Conrad are getting more active. On

Sunday mornings, for example, they have a light breakfast and go mountain biking instead of doing brunch.

How to Show Love without Food

ONCE YOU'VE RECOGNIZED that excessively expressing love with food is a problem in your relationship, you can start taking steps to move away from it.

1. Exchange What's Your Relationship To Food? quizzes and talk through each response.
2. List all the reasons you love your partner that have nothing to do with food or culinary skills. Then list all the non-food items or activities you enjoy as much as food. For example, you might name CDs, books, or a favor like a back rub or ironing your clothes. Give your partner both lists so he or she knows other ways to treat you.
3. Before looking at each other's lists, write down some ways you can express your feelings without food. Then compare lists and refer to them when you want to do something special.

Partners can also compromise here and work out a schedule for the indulgences that makes them both comfortable. If one partner feels that just once a month is not realistic, find a happy medium. Explore taking the element of surprise out of the treats. In Conrad and Sarah's case, for example, if Conrad consults Sarah before he makes a dessert, she can objectively decide if she wants to indulge, before a tempting cake or pie is in front of her.

Outside help is also crucial here and involves expanding the support network. I referred Conrad to a psychotherapist who does a lot of work looking at how childhood family dynamics impact adult relationships. Conrad just scratched the surface of some family issues and a psychotherapist could really help him delve further into them. Therapy could have a tremendously positive impact on Conrad and Sarah's relationship and help with the food issues we touched on.

Sarah is thrilled about the changes they've made. She started losing weight and she and Conrad are getting more active. On Sunday mornings, for example, they have a light breakfast and go mountain biking instead of doing brunch.

Using food as a replacement for love is a hard habit to break, so I won't be surprised if I see one or both of these two again. They won't solve this issue overnight, but awareness is a huge step toward better health. Acknowledging this issue early on dramatically increases their chances of having a good relationship and better health.

Therapy Help

TO FIND A therapist, contact the American Psychological Association at www.apa.org.

12

I Need Help
with this Diagnosis

DEALING WITH A HEALTH CONDITION THAT
CHANGES THE HOUSEHOLD DIET

Patrick, a forty-two-year-old busy insurance agent, never thought much about cholesterol. But when some coworkers got tested at a company sponsored health fair, he thought, "What the heck." He was shocked when the nurse told him his results showed that he was at high risk for heart disease. "You should follow up with your physician right away," she advised.

When Patrick came home, his wife Lillian, forty-one, was making cheeseburgers for dinner. "No more cheeseburgers," he said, tossing the test result form on the countertop. Lillian reassured him, but couldn't help thinking, "Why should I have to give up burgers, too?" Lillian had always been one of the lucky ones who could eat whatever she wanted to without gaining weight or suffering from health problems.

Patrick saw his doctor the next week. Afterwards, he told his wife how Dr. Webber wanted to do more tests, start some medications, and send him to a dietitian.

"I feel so overwhelmed." he said, shaking his head.

"Don't worry," Lillian said. "I'll go with you and find out how I can help."

At first, the fact that Lillian wanted to participate didn't make sense to him. Growing up, his mother had diabetes but his father never had anything to do with it. Her health was her deal. In fact, his dad didn't know anything about how to help with the disease until she got much worse and he had to give her insulin shots. But Lillian's so good at this stuff, Patrick thought, and then agreed to let her come.

Partners of people with any medical condition are an integral part of managing the condition. There's so much a partner can do to support someone during a diagnosis. A partner can remain objective and unemotional if the other is having a hard time accepting the diagnosis. Partners are in a better position to remain positive and learn all they can. Most of all, they can help their partner reconnect with who they are and plan something they know will make them laugh or take their mind off the diagnosis. Down the road, partners can continue to play an important supportive role. By keeping up on the other person's health status without nagging, asking how appointments went, reviewing test results, and encouraging daily or weekly exercise goals, partners can keep others on track. And they can continue to make their significant other feel that the diagnosis is not his or her life but, rather, an aspect of it.

Because couples grocery shop together for each other, cook together, dine together, trust each other, and know each other so well, when one partner has a condition requiring special care, the other should be thoroughly educated about it.

Years ago, it would have been common for a woman with diabetes to keep her husband at arm's length or even totally in the dark about her treatment or any other aspect of her other health care issues. Often, a spouse wouldn't know the specifics of the condition until it developed into a serious health problem. Today, however, doctors and other care providers realize how much a significant other can help, and actually encourage partners to get involved.

After a medical diagnosis, a significant other's concerned attitude and willingness to participate in their care can empower the other partner and ease his or her worries. Any medical problem—whether it's high cholesterol, a food allergy, or high blood pressure—requires a change in lifestyle. And because couples share that lifestyle, the most effective way to change is as a team.

I've seen many individuals leave a health care provider's offices informed and motivated. But once they actually have to put their new knowledge into practice, a partner's *support*—or lack of support—makes all the difference. That's why asking your partner to not only understand your problem—but to help you deal with it—is one of the best things you can do for your health.

Imagine you've just been diagnosed with high cholesterol. Your doctor has explained what this means and prescribed a new drug for you. You've been given a great deal of new information about reading food labels, substituting ingredients in home cooked meals, ordering differently at restaurants, managing your stress level, and increasing your physical activity. A week later you're at the drug store picking up your prescription. The pharmacist tells you to take this medication with a glass of water and avoid alcohol. You wish your partner was there so that later on, he or she will understand why you can't split a bottle of Merlot at dinner anymore.

A few hours later you're in the grocery store together. It's taking a lot longer than normal because you're scouring the store for whole wheat pasta and canola oil—foods you've never purchased before. You can't quite remember what the dietitian taught you about reading the food label. You wish you could ask your partner but he or she wasn't there to hear the guidelines and instructions.

The next day, the two of you stop at the food court to grab a bite while shopping. You'd normally head straight for A&W for a chili dog and root beer, your favorite mall meal, but you know that's out of the question now. You stand there, scanning the Chinese noodles, pizza, burgers, tacos, subs, and other options, wishing someone could help you figure out what to order. But when you ask your partner for help, you hear, "One meal isn't going to matter, just get what you want." That evening, feeling a little guilty about the fact that the only vegetable you consumed today was the sauce on your slice of cheese pizza, you think about going for a walk around the neighborhood. You remember that the dietitian recommended getting a pedometer and using it to set activity goals. You walk into the living room and there's your spouse, sitting in front of the TV, one hand on the remote, the other in a bag of Doritos. You feel alone and overwhelmed and it's easier to give in and join him/her. "Oh, well," you think, as you plop down on the couch, "at least I'm on medication. That should help."

Unfortunately, this scenario plays out over and over across America. Lack of partner support is one big reason we aren't more successful at battling obesity and chronic diseases like heart disease and diabetes. When told to change their lifestyle, most people feel it's just as impossible as climbing Mt. Everest. Many couples have found a lifestyle comfort zone, and changing that is difficult. However, if you work together, it is not unachievable. "Lifestyle changes" generally mean altering behaviors such as eating, physical activity, sleeping, drinking alcohol, and stress management. These activities are undoubtedly intertwined with your relationship. Your partner doesn't have to go jogging with you to support you—but you are more likely to exercise on a regular basis if he or she cheers you on your way out the door or asks you how your workout was. The decisions you make about where, when, and what to eat, whether or not to exercise, how much, how often, and what you drink, when to go to sleep and wake up, and how to handle everyday and chronic stress are strongly influenced by your partner's preferences, behaviors, and overall attitude.

For example, while my husband was in graduate school he worked at night. I worked during the day. He got home from work around 2:00 A.M.—four hours before I had to get up. I always had trouble falling asleep when he wasn't home. I'd often wait up for him and if I did doze off, I'd wake up when he got home, sometimes staying up for a full hour to talk. Needless to say, this had serious ramifications on the quantity and quality of my sleep. My energy level dragged all week then I'd sleep away half of Saturday, feeling like I'd wasted my day off. It was impossible for me to meet my goal of securing the six to eight sleep hours I needed each night. His lifestyle—specifically, his work and sleep schedule—really interfered with my health goal. Luckily for us, it was only temporary.

Dietary changes are no different. The best thing that the partner of someone newly diagnosed with a health condition can do is treat it as not "her" or "his" problem but as "our" problem. For example, it's not enough to know that a partner with diabetes should avoid sugary foods. It's not just what is consumed, but how much and at what time that matters. To help, you need to learn about the disease in depth, really comprehend what diabetes means, and understand how nutrition can positively or negatively impact it. You'll need to learn understand your partner's specific diet prescription, which means attending appointments, learning how to read food labels, getting educated about portion sizes, altering recipes, and planning ahead when dining out. You need to be his or her cheerleader, confidant, support system and coach. After all, you'd expect the same from your partner if the shoe was on the other foot. Simple things like knowing what goals your partner is working on for the day or week, sharing encouraging words, offering to do the laundry so he or she can get on the treadmill, or just asking how you can help will make all the difference.

Want to Help a Partner with a Newly Diagnosed Medical Condition Make Dietary Changes?

GET INVOLVED. ATTEND doctor and dietitian appointments, get informed about the disease, learn how to read food labels and measure portion sizes, help with cooking and shopping, and be supportive of his or her dietary goals all the time—when dining out, on weekends, vacations, and holidays.

HOW TO ASK YOUR PARTNER FOR HELP

If you aren't getting as much support as you need, verbally ask for help. Tell your partner how you're feeling, whether you're scared, overwhelmed, or anxious. Then explain that you really need their help. Try to remember an example of a difficult time he or she went through when your help was required. If it's unlikely that your partner will be able to help as much as you'd like, list about three to five concrete examples of ways you'd like him or her to help. If your partner cannot attend every medical or nutrition appointment, ask if he or she can attend the crucial ones or set aside a time to talk each week to discuss your goals and challenges.

Seeking a Support Group?

FIND ONE NEAR you on the relevant condition site:

www.diabetes.org
www.americanheart.org
www.cancer.org
www.celiac.org
www.ccfa.org
www.foodallergy.org

If you're flying solo and your partner won't get involved in your health care, ask your doctor to prompt him or her into helping out. If that doesn't work, a friend or relative can pick up the slack by joining a support group for family members of people with the condition.

Patrick eventually made peace with his diagnosis. In the beginning, Lillian helped him out by sitting in on doctor's appoinments and taking notes that he could review later. She did Internet research and printed out information so they could both learn about high cholesterol. Now she understands enough to help him navigate restaurant menus, encourage him to make healthy choices, and continue to control his cholesterol. Patrick's condition actually brought this couple closer and helped them realize just how crucial their partnership is. "My cholesterol has come down by fifty points," he bragged, "but I never could have done this well on my own." In fact, Patrick's cholesterol even started a new tradition. Every Friday night, he and Lillian look at photos from places they've visited—Europe, Asia, Hawaii, the Caribbean—and discuss the memorable dishes they shared. Then, on Sunday night, they re-create heart healthy versions at home. The delicious pasta with meat sauce they shared in Florence morphed into whole-wheat angel hair pasta with chunky marinara and ground turkey. Over time, they've even grown to love the lighter versions better.

13

Can You Help Me Finish This?

WHAT TO DO WHEN ONE PARTNER ENCOURAGES
THE OTHER TO OVEREAT

 Susie and Jane have been together for years, own
an antiques business together, and make a fantastic team.
Susie, twenty-eight, loves to eat but physically is petite.
Jane, thirty, has a medium build, and shares Susie's love for food. When they
go out, Susie's eyes are bigger than her stomach. She gets excited about
creamy artichoke dip or crème brulee and encourages Jane to indulge with
her, whether or not she's hungry. As they browse menus, Susie will ask, "Can
you help me with this?" Or, after her plate is on the table, "Can you finish this
for me?" Jane hates to waste food as much as Susie does, but as the same
time she feels like Susie's garbage disposal.

Jane called me after she saw a television segment I did on couples' food conflicts. I listened to her problem and asked, "Have
you told Susie how you feel?" Not surprisingly, she hadn't.

"I wasn't sure it was a real problem, and I didn't want to start
a fight," she explained. "We never argue so it feels weird to bring
this up."

I asked Jane if she and her partner had any other food issues or nutrition questions. She said neither of them have major weight or health concerns but they are active, enjoy biking and hiking, and are always interested in learning more about eating for endurance. I suggested they come in together to talk about that and take it from there.

Jane and Susie came in eager to learn about fueling their outdoor endeavors. After reviewing sports drinks and comparing energy bars, I gently asked if they had any additional food related issues. "Well," Jane said hesitantly. "Sometimes we have trouble when we eat out."

Susie, surprised, asked, "What do you mean?"

Jane looked back and forth between Susie and me. "Well, sometimes I feel like you want me to eat things with you or finish what you order even when I say I'm not hungry."

"Really?" Susie seemed genuinely taken aback.

She may not have realized it, but Jane had just put the SANITY model into play. By honestly bringing up her concerns in the security of a professional office, she asked Susie to be candid as well, opened the door to communication, and took a vital first step toward resolving their food clash.

While Susie was a bit uncomfortable hearing this for the first time in front of a stranger, she was concerned, not defensive. To keep the discussion going, I explained that issues like this are extremely common. I asked Susie if she felt Jane's concern was valid.

"Yes, I guess I do that." She paused for a moment, "But I thought it was just fun for both of us. I didn't realize Jane saw it as a problem."

I asked Jane to elaborate. She told Susie she does enjoy dining out but she often feels pressured into eating things she normally wouldn't, or more than she'd like to. Because of Susie's prompting, she often leaves a restaurant feeling sluggish and bloated, while Susie is energized.

I asked Jane to give a specific example.

"Remember the last time we went to the Cheesecake Factory and you said you wanted to try the avocado egg rolls?" Jane explained. "I said I'd rather save room for dessert. You said, 'Oh come on, let's splurge and get both.' And after they came out you ate half of one and then kept saying, 'Eat those so they don't go to waste.' When the cheesecake came out, I said I was already full. You insisted we had to eat it because we weren't going home and couldn't wrap it up. You kept pushing the plate toward me."

Susie was silent, processing.

I stepped in. "Jane, it sounds like you feel you have to take on a lot of responsibility in these situations, is that right?"

She nodded and Susie, with tears starting to fill up her eyes, said, "Jane, I'm sorry. I didn't realize I was putting that on you. I wish you would have told me."

With a little more probing Susie recognized that her behavior was really motivated by her own inability to limit her intake. When she can't decide between two things, she asks Jane to share. Or if she wants just a taste of a dessert, she asks Jane to order it. It's almost like a mind game: if Susie doesn't order dessert herself, it doesn't "count." But if they share it, Susie can literally have her cake and eat it too—feel "good" about not eating as much, and avoid feeling deprived at the same time. This way, Susie passes the responsibility for the dessert onto Jane, which in this case, means taking care of it or finishing it.

In my office, Susie was able to recognize that she has control issues with food. Her mother was a perpetual dieter who weighed and measured her food, counted calories, and strictly avoided "forbidden" foods, like the cakes she baked for Susie's birthdays. As an adult, Susie was determined not to ride the diet rollercoaster. She knew it was not realistic to go through her life depriving herself of foods she loved. However, she didn't fully trust herself around food. She always worried about losing control and overeating. Indulging with Jane was like using a safety net. She could eat the foods she loved without being solely responsible for making decisions about ordering or finishing risky foods. This took the pressure and guilt off Susie's shoulders.

I congratulated Jane and Susie for talking openly and told them about the SANITY model couples can use to work through problems like these. The most important ones here are seeing conflicts honestly and asking each other to understand.

To help them be honest, I suggested Jane and Susie use the Y SANITY step and yuck it up with some humor. Their homework assignment was to come up with a silly signal—a funny phrase, nickname, body language, or even a facial expression that made the other smile. They were then to use the silly signal as a way to loosen up, open lines of communication, and begin a calm dialogue. Jane promised to use this technique the next time Susie did something that made her feel pressured.

Alternatively, she could say something like this, "Remember how we promised to be honest with each other about our food issues? Well, I'm feeling a little pressured right now. Can we talk about it?"

Susie agreed to be more aware of her sometimes pushy food behavior and listen to Jane when she feels her own dominating nature slip out.

Over the years, many couples have told me, "We don't fight about money, or politics, or what to do on the weekends. Our only tension revolves around food." Some couples are so compatible, so used to smooth sailing, they have no experience dealing with disagreement. When a food conflict arises they don't know how to handle it.

Susie may have been a bully with food, but she generally respects Jane's wishes. She never pushes her to rent the movie she'd prefer or paint the living room her favorite color. Because of this, Jane had no real experience confronting Susie. Now that they've uncovered and acknowledged this issue, they are developing skills and tools to deal with other stumbling blocks. I'm confident that this pair will be just fine food-wise.

If you're flying solo on this, find ways to politely refuse excess portions along with a practical explanation your food intimidator will accept. When someone says, "No, thanks. I'm full," others often dismiss this as a non-excuse, responding with, "Oh, come on," or "You hardly ate anything."

How to Fight Off a Food Pusher

FEELING PRESSURED? Deflect a food bully with these rock solid reasons why you can't have anymore.

- "No, thanks. I have a hard time sleeping if I eat too much."
- "Thanks, but I have to pass. I get bad heartburn if I overeat."
- "No, thank you. When I'm too full I get sleepy and I have to drive home."
- "I wish I could, but my doctor recommended I eat smaller, more frequent meals to better control my blood sugar."

If all else fails, consent to a small bite. Often just the tiniest taste can satisfy the biggest food bully.

14

It's So Unfair! You Can Eat Anything and Never Gain an Ounce!

BUILDING A HEALTHY BODY IMAGE WHEN YOU LIVE WITH A LEAN MACHINE

Shelby, twenty-three, feels like her husband Adam, twenty-five, can eat anything and burn it right off, while she gains five pounds just looking at a piece of cake. To her dismay, she fell in love with a tall, wiry, and small-boned man. She wishes she was that petite. All of the women in Shelby's family are voluptuous, average height, and large framed, and Shelby is no exception. Ever since she was a teen, she has struggled with her body image. Living with Adam has not improved her self-image. He comes from a long line of lean men who can eat all day and night without ever gaining weight. Adam has even tried to bulk up. He ate extra shakes, peanut butter sandwiches, and bagels, but only gained three pounds. Ultimately, he threw in the towel and resumed his intuitive eating patterns. Adam's huge appetite and his magical ability to eat anything and everything drives Shelby insane.

"Where does it all go?" she wonders. "Does he have a tape worm?"

She carefully avoids the chips, nuts, dressings, cookies, and sodas he consumes so carelessly. It frustrates her to watch him eat this way, and upsets her that high-fat, high-calorie foods are always in the house.

Unfortunately, we cannot choose our genetics. If Shelby continues to compare herself to an ideal unrealistic for her body, she will always feel frustrated. Even worse, she will never achieve a healthy relationship with food. While Adam's thinness may be difficult for Shelby to take, he cannot change his natural lean tendency. Unlike his wife, Adam has come to accept this fact along with his leanness.

In cases like this, where one partner envies the other's metabolism, the solution primarily lies with the person who's not blessed with lean genes. Shelby must explore her feelings and figure out how to make peace with food and her body.

The following *honesty* worksheet can help uncover the ways of thinking that can damage body image. After answering these questions honestly, take at least fifteen minutes to reread your response and reflect.

Do You Have any Destructive Food Attitudes?

QUESTION	RESPONSE
Please describe your relationship with food.	
Do you categorize foods as good and bad? If so, what determines a "good" or "bad" food?	
How do your feelings about your body impact the way you eat?	
How do you determine when to eat?	
How do you determine what to eat?	
How do you determine when to stop?	
If you were not concerned about your weight, would you eat differently?	
What have you learned about food from your childhood caregivers?	
What is your description of a "normal" eater?	
What is your description of a "dysfunctional" eater?	
What type of eater do you think you are?	
How would you like to change your eating habits, or relationship with food? Please respond without referring to your weight.	

And here are Shelby's responses:

Do You Have any Destructive Food Attitudes?

QUESTION	RESPONSE
Please describe your relationship with food.	*Awful. I feel guilty eating practically anything. Food is not my friend!*
Do you categorize foods as good and bad? If so, what determines a "good" or "bad" food?	*Yes! I guess the criteria include calorie level, fat level, carb level, and whatever I've heard is fattening or not fattening.*
How do your feelings about your body impact the way you eat?	*It drives the way I eat. If I'm having a "fat" day, I either try to be really good or I get so discouraged that I give up and eat whatever I want (then feel super guilty afterward).*
How do you determine when to eat?	*I never thought about that before. I guess when it's time, like breakfast, lunch, dinner, but also based on what other people are doing. For example, if everyone at work is having a snack, I usually have something.*
How do you determine what to eat?	*Either what I think I should eat (to lose weight) or sometimes what I want (with guilt).*
How do you determine when to stop?	*Again, a question I haven't thought much about. I guess when it's gone.*
If you were not concerned about your weight, would you eat differently?	*Yes! No doubt! I'd eat all the foods Adam can eat without feeling guilty!*
What have you learned about food from your childhood caregivers?	*A lot about dieting. It's a standard topic of conversation among the women in my family.*
What is your description of a "normal" eater?	*I have no idea! I guess Adam is a normal eater.*

What is your description of a "dysfunctional" eater?	*Me! I spend too much time thinking about food.*
What type of eater do you think you are?	*Definitely dysfunctional but it's all I've ever known.*
How would you like to change your eating habits, or relationship with food? Please respond without referring to your weight.	*Gosh, it's hard for me to take weight out of the equation. Food and weight are linked in my mind.*

YOUR PERSONAL FOOD ROOM

Here's where using your imagination to find new solutions works well. The following *creativity* exercise helps illustrate relationships with food. It's a great tool to start making peace with food. Use a pen and paper and take your time. Visualize a solid door five feet in front of you. Picture its size, color, and texture. In your dominant hand, you hold a key to this door. Visualize the key. You hold the only key to this door. Feeling relaxed and calm, imagine slowly walking toward the door. Insert the key and step into your personal food room. The door will shut behind you and no one else will be able to enter. There are no windows in your personal food room and no cameras. Nobody can see you or judge you. When you are in this room time stands still. You can take as much time as you like without worrying about getting back to your world. Look around you. Every food you've ever known of is in this room. It is all fresh and magically, when you take something, another portion replaces it so you never run out of any item. Before touching anything, look around the room. Take a deep breath and check in with your thoughts and feelings. What are you thinking? What are you feeling? Take a moment to write down your responses. Be sure to distinguish between thoughts and feelings. Feelings can usually be described in one word, a variation of happy, angry, sad or, afraid. Thoughts are more wordy descriptions, i.e., "I was thinking about all the work I have to do." Take another look around the room. Tell yourself that you can come back to this room any time you'd like to. It's your personal food room. Be sure you have the key in your hand and exit the room.

The thoughts and feelings people experience in the food room indicate their relationships with food. Those who feel calm and at peace in the room probably have a healthy rapport with food. For this group, food is not connected to emotions, self-esteem, or self-judgment.

Like many people—and women in particular—Shelby felt anxious in the room and did not feel calm or peace. She was unsure of herself, and hesitant to choose the wrong thing. She was also afraid that she would lose control. If you were uncomfortable in the room, see the interpretations of food room feelings below.

WHAT YOUR FOOD ROOM FEELINGS MEAN

FEELING: *Fear, anxiety, discomfort*
INTERPRETATION: If these feelings surfaced while you were in the food room, ask yourself why. Are you afraid to be around the food because you may lose control? Do you not trust yourself enough to be around the food without worrying you will do something wrong? What is the fear or anxiety related to? Is it tied to a fear of gaining weight? If you experience these feelings, food represents much more to you than a means of nourishing your body. When food choices are linked to feelings of self-esteem or self-worth, food becomes a focal point of everyday life. Consider reading *Intuitive Eating* by Evelyn Tribole, MS, RD, and Alyse Resch, MS, RD Talking to a registered dietitian who specializes in disordered or dysfunctional eating can also help you work through these issues. As you work on disconnecting food and emotions, revisit the food room to find out if your feelings change.

FEELING: *Calm, at peace, relaxed*
INTERPRETATION: If you felt calm inside the food room, ask

yourself what this feeling was related to? Did it feel good to know that the food was yours and could not be taken away from you? Did you feel at peace because nobody could watch or judge you, or did you feel relaxed simply because to you, food is just food? Understanding why we feel the way we do is key to analyzing our relationship with food. If your feelings of calm surprised you, ask yourself what it was about this room that allowed you to feel that way. When you are faced with food choices, remember this experience and allow it to help you make decisions.

This exercise is powerful because it can alter the way we look at food. In many ways, the room is real. Most of us do have incredible access to food. For most adults, there is no food that will fly off the face of the Earth never to be seen again. It's never the "last chance" to have something because there will always be another opportunity. Chronic dieters often feel they have to "get enough" of certain foods when they can because as soon as they go back on the diet they will not be allowed to have this food. This "all or nothing" thinking gives food a great deal of power over us. We're compelled to have certain foods because they are forbidden or special. In reality there is no food that is inherently bad or fattening. Food is only stored as fat if we eat more calories than we can use. A great deal of nutrition science supports this. Do you believe this, or are you hanging on to an irrational set of food "rules" that cloud your feelings? What would happen if you let go of the good/bad, right/wrong food thinking? If you truly believed that no food was "bad," would it change how you feel about food and how you eat?

CHILDISH RELATIONSHIPS WITH FOOD

Most small children have incredibly healthy relationships with food. Toddlers have not yet developed strong ties between food and emotions or food and society. They tend to eat when they are hungry, enjoy their meal, and stop when they've had enough. For example, you'd never hear a toddler say:

- I really shouldn't be eating that.
- I've been so "bad" today, I'll have to be "good" tomorrow.
- I had such a bad day I want to drown my sorrows in a pint of Ben & Jerry's.
- I can't have cookies in the house because I might lose control and eat them all.
- I can't have that, I'm on a diet.

Even thinking about small children talking this way seems silly or sad. Yet, this is reality for many grown men and women. If you can stop using unhealthy dieting rules to judge your food decisions, you'll feel better about food. Without judgment, it's possible to make choices based on what feels right at the moment versus what you "should" do.

See Food through a Child's Eyes

IMAGINE WHAT IT would be like to approach food the way a toddler does. What would he or she think or feel in the personal food room?

Kids' Positive Food Attitudes

A toddler decides when to eat, what to eat, and when to stop based on what creates the best sense of well-being. If you've ever cared for small children you'll recognize their straigh forward relationships with food.

- Kids tell you when they are hungry. They don't mistake true physical hunger from emotional hunger because they have other ways of dealing with emotions, such as crying, having a temper tantrum, or playing.

◆ They tell you exactly what they want and are very in tune with what feels right at the moment. They say, "No, I don't want milk, I want juice!"

◆ Young kids stop eating and/or drinking when they feel they've had enough, despite what's left on the plate or in the glass.

◆ They enjoy food, often making "Mmmmm" sounds, smiling or expressing how "yummy" their food is.

◆ It's nearly impossible to get a toddler to eat when he or she doesn't want to. They may say no, turn their head, play with the food, spit it out, or throw it at you!

What holds you back from having this kind of relationship with food? Looking at food like a toddler can free us from fear, anxiety, and guilt. Many us of are trapped by food rules, we believe we can't eat anything we like if we're trying to lose weight, or that we should get our money's worth even if it means overeating. A lot of people feel compelled to clean their plate or accept any food that's offered because turning it down would be impolite. If you have a set of rules that govern your eating decisions, explore them with the following chart.

How Do Your Food Rules Influence You?

RULE	ORIGIN OF RULE	PROBLEMS THIS RULE HAS CAUSED FOR ME	ALTERNATIVES TO THIS RULE

Here are a few of Shelby's rules:

How Do Your Food Rules Influence You?

RULE	ORIGIN OF RULE	PROBLEMS THIS RULE HAS CAUSED FOR ME	ALTERNATIVES TO THIS RULE
Avoid "bad" foods	My family and many dieting women friends who have passed these rules on to me	I feel deprived, get increased cravings. I know it's not realistic to never have certain foods. I feel incredibly guilty when I have something I think I shouldn't. I get in a bad mood because of this. It interferes with my relationship with Adam.	I could start thinking like the toddler, eating something if I'm hungry, trying to enjoy it and stopping when I've had enough. This seems strange but I do see my nieces and nephews eating this way. Maybe I can go back to this!
Eat when it's time	My family/society/ schedule	Sometimes I eat when I'm not hungry which could be related to not being able to lose weight	I guess I could try not eating if I'm not hungry because I can always stop and have a snack if I need to.

These exercises helped Shelby realize that her food paradigm was unrealistic and unnatural. I reinforced that there are no good and no bad foods. No food is off limits, even to those trying to lose weight. Our bodies need a certain amount of calories every day. Those calories are made up of carbohydrates, protein, and fat. Each of these essential nutrients are required to achieve and maintain a healthy ideal weight. Therefore, even as Shelby reduces her total calorie intake to the amount needed to support her ideal weight, she has a certain "budget" per day to spend on each type of calorie.

THINK ABOUT THE BIG FOOD PICTURE

If Shelby chooses to spend her daily fat budget on a few high-fat foods such as peanut butter, cheese, and salad dressing, she can balance the budget by consuming low-fat foods like vegetables, fruits, and lean proteins for the rest of the day. The same is true for carbohydrates and protein. Long-term weight loss and healthy weight maintenance is all about balance. Consuming less carbs, protein, or fat than the body needs can actually stall weight loss. Too few nutrients can create deficits that slow down metabolism, diminish muscle tissue, or create other adverse effects like a weakened immune system. This "big picture" perspective combined with a thorough understanding of human metabolism prompts dietitians to declare that no food needs to be eliminated.

Once Shelby begins to look at food in this way, she could free herself from the problematic thinking that prevents her from being a "normal" eater.

Shelby's homework assignment was to go through one day eating in response to her body's natural instincts, rather than any strict food rules. Once she completed this task, she was amazed at how letting go of her food rules changed her eating. She found that she wasn't compelled to eat something just because Adam was. A few times she started eating something, realized it wasn't very satisfying and stopped. She put it down because she wanted to, not because she thought she should.

In many cases, once strict rules are removed and the "budget" outlook is adopted, people tune into their natural eating instincts, and choose a healthy balance. In thinking about your own body's natural instincts, not rules, try to stayed tuned into your body for twenty-four hours. Ask yourself these questions throughout the day.

1. When you think about food, check in with your body. Do you have physical symptoms of hunger?

2. If no, what are you thinking and/or feeling? How can you address those thoughts and feelings without food?
3. If you are hungry, what do you really want to eat? Think about taste, texture, temperature, seasoning, etc.
4. How can I eat what I want in a way that will feel good while I am eating it, leave me full but not overly full, and make me satisfied and energized?

HOW A LEAN PARTNER CAN HELP A LOVED ONE MAKE PEACE WITH FOOD

Partners can help make our environment more positive. Shelby gave Adam this handout and asked for his support in helping her let go of her destructive food attitudes.

You can't change your metabolism, but you can change your attitude. Here are a few ways to be as supportive as possible:

◆ Remind your partner that you love him or her just the way she is.
◆ Ask her what you can do to help. It might be easier if you don't offer snacks when you're eating. Refrain from commenting on what or how much your partner is eating.
◆ If you consider trying to gain weight, seek professional help. Quick fix products on the market may hurt your health and your wallet. In order to gain muscle mass, proper nutrition must be combined with a well-designed weight training program. Consult with a well-qualified exercise professional, preferably a personal trainer with a degree in exercise physiology and a recognized certification, such as ACSM, the American College of Sports Medicine, as well as with a registered dietitian with experience in sports nutrition. To find a qualified trainer near you, visit www.acsm.org.

Beginning to make peace with food has allowed Shelby to accept the differences between her body and Adam's body. She no longer compares herself to him or gets angry with him for being able to eat more food. The tension between them has eased. As Shelby begins to feel better about herself without being trapped in food prison, her body image has improved. And that's made everything else, from their sex life to her job confidence, better.

15

I Deserve a Donut!

EMOTIONAL EATING AND COMFORT FOODS

 Kevin, forty, recently suffered the loss of his mother and underwent a job change. About six months ago, his wife Kelly, thirty-three, noticed that he was dealing with his emotions by eating. Almost every night, Kevin would come home from work, consume a large meal, and then raid the cupboards, mindlessly downing chocolate chip cookies, peanut M&Ms, and pints of Ben & Jerry's Chocolate Fudge Brownie ice cream. Kelly was conflicted. At first, she thought it best not to interfere; eventually his behavior would pass.

"I want to help but I don't want to patrol his eating habits or make him feel any worse," she said when she called me for advice. But lately, Kevin has gained weight, complains of constant fatigue, heartburn, and insomnia. "How can I be supportive without badgering him?"

Kevin, like many of us, has learned that food provides a diversion from our feelings. We can stuff down emotions with food and temporarily escape bad feelings by eating. When sad or depressed, people often crave comfort foods and/or high carbohydrate foods to sooth themselves. Comfort foods are typically foods we remember from childhood, things caregivers provided, familiar foods, cultural foods, or things that make us feel closer to our roots. These foods help us feel safe, or, as some of my clients say, like you're giving yourself a hug.

Kelly had offhandedly asked her husband about his evening eating in the past, but he'd shrugged the question off and said that he was just snacking because he was bored. I explained to Kelly that boredom isn't really the reason most people eat. They may think they are bored when they are really experiencing another emotion that's driving them to eat, like loneliness. Feeling bored is often a signal that there are other issues under the surface. Well-adjusted people with rich social lives rarely feel bored. They spend down time reaching out to friends, working on hobbies or projects or embarking on new adventures. Feeling bored can be a sign that someone has become socially isolated, lacks balance between their personal and professional lives, or is suffering from depression.

Everyone uses food for emotional reasons from time to time. I grew up in Upstate New York, in apple country, and after I moved to Florida, I had serious candy apple cravings every fall. I once drove over an hour to Orlando to buy one. It was apple season, and I was homesick. The Florida sun was so hot that it melted the candy coating all over my shirt and shoes, but I was so happy I didn't care!

Kevin's case, however, is beyond homesickness. It's serious and calls for professional help. Counselors believe that people like Kevin use food when they are depressed because it provides a sense of security when our lives become chaotic or out of our control. Research shows that consuming carbohydrates when we are upset produces a chemical reaction in our brains that induces calm[3, 4]. And emotional eating is often learned. As kids,

---

[3] Dallman, et al. "Chronic Stress and Obsesity: A New View of 'Comfort Food.'" PNAS, 100, no. 20 (2003): 11696–11701.

[4] Bruinsma, K. and D.L. Taren. "Chocolate: Food or Drug?" *Jouranl of the American Dietetic Association*, 99, no. 10 (1999): 1249–1256.

we observe adults eating to satisfy emotions, and sometimes this type of eating is imposed upon us. Parents may take a child to McDonald's, as a reward for being brave in the doctor's office, or grandparents may slip caramels into children's pockets to show love. Nearly every client I've seen can remember getting food as a reward for an accomplishment (an exceptional report card or good deed), or in consolation (after a skinned knee, bad day at school, or not making the team). On top of the biochemical and learned reasons we use food for comfort, certain food textures can help us address various feelings. When we're angry, we can take out our aggressions on crunchy pretzels, chips, or chewy licorice. When we're feeling blue, we can soothe ourselves with rich gooey chocolate, or creamy soft ice cream.

Chapter Five introduced the triangle that illustrates how thoughts, feelings, and behaviors are connected. The triangle also applies here. By definition, emotional eating is coping with thoughts and feelings by eating, instead of addressing them directly. When this happens, it's important to deal with the underlying thoughts and feelings as well as the behavior (the emotional eating). Failing to sort through the thoughts and feelings that cause the emotional eating can result in more eating, despite the desire to stop, or redirecting them toward another destructive behavior like compulsive shopping, excessive alcohol consumption, drug usage, or becoming a workaholic.

After I spoke with Kelly she decided to gently approach Kevin. The following tips can help the partner of an emotional eater open the lines of communication:

HOW TO APPROACH A PARTNER
WHO'S USING FOOD FOR COMFORT

Remember that this is an emotional issue, not simply a bad habit. Be sensitive and gentle.

- Find a time to approach to your partner when you will have adequate time to talk and will not be interrupted. Do not disrupt your partner when he/she is busy working, sleeping, or eating.

- Ask your partner if you can talk to him/her about something that's important to you. Don't start the conversation with a statement such as, "I need to talk to you about your eating." Accusations may put your partner on the defense or alarm him or her.

- Start out with a loving statement such as, "I care about you so much and I know it's been a difficult time for you."

- Follow the statement by addressing your partner's behavior without using accusatory or critical statements. Instead of saying, "You've been eating a lot lately," or "You're gaining weight," word your concerns in a way that focus less on the behavior and more on the person. For example, " I'm concerned that you have a lot of feelings bottled up inside. I've noticed some changes in your behavior lately and I want to be there for you," or "You seem upset. Are you okay?"

- Reinforce that you are not accusing anyone of doing anything wrong. Explain how difficult it is for you to see him or her hurting and that you want to provide support. You might convey this by saying something like, "I'm worried about you because you don't seem happy. I want to help you if I can."

- Hopefully your partner will feel safe enough to begin an honesty dialogue with you. However, he or she may not be ready. If your partner remains closed off or noncommunicative, accept the fact that he or she is not ready to confront these issues. At this point, seek out outside resources to help you deal with your feelings and accept that it is not your role or duty to "fix" your partner. Talk to a supportive friend or someone who's going through a similar situation.

Fortunately, Kevin was ready to discuss his feelings with Kelly and was grateful for her concern. He shifted his weight in his chair—he was a bit ashamed and embarrassed at being called out by Kelly, even as gently as she went about confronting him. Kevin knew he was depressed and had started to realize that he couldn't just will it away. When she suggested professional counseling Kevin agreed that it was the best course of action.

TO FIND A counselor, go to the website of the American Psychological Association: www.apa.org.

While it is difficult to stand by and watch a loved one participate in an unhealthy pattern of eating, disordered eating cannot by solved by a significant other. Nothing can be done until the person struggling with it becomes aware that it's a problem, and is ready to receive help.

Kevin began seeing a therapist to work through the grief and other emotional issues he had been experiencing. When ignored, feelings like grief tend to surface in the form of disordered eating, high blood pressure, or digestive upset like nausea, constipation, diarrhea, or acidy stomach. In some cases, addressing the underlying issues will resolve chaotic eating behaviors, and the eater will resume his or her previous natural eating patterns. This occurs when the individual finds other coping mechanism and no longer "needs" food. In other cases, additional nutrition counseling can help a client get back on track. In these cases, the person receives mental health counseling as well as nutritional counseling.

Sometimes I use a shipwreck analogy to help explain how the different types of counseling compliment each other. An emotional eater is like a castaway who has been alone on an island for a long time. The mental-health work helps the person get back home while the nutrition work helps him or her relearn the language.

When someone like Kevin has started to work on the underlying issues and is ready to resume "normal" eating, I often ask him or her to keep a food journal. While it tracks what and when her or she eats, the purpose of the journal is really to examine how and why he or she is eating. An example of a journal is below:

Food Journal

ITEM	RESPONSE
Time of meal or snack.	A.M. P.M.
Where was meal or snack consumed?	
Did you eat alone or with someone else?	
Were you aware of being physically hungry when you began eating?	
If not, were you aware of any other emotions, or thoughts, such as boredom, anger, loneliness, depression, etc.	
How did you decide what to eat?	
How did you feel when you were finished eating? Were you full, not full, or overly full? Were you satisfied? Were you energized or did you experience a lack of energy after consuming this meal or snack?	
How did you decide when to stop eating?	
If you could re-do this meal to produce a better outcome, what would you have done differently if anything?	

By thinking through these issues, clients get in tune with body signals, identify patterns, connect what they eat to how and why they eat, and begin making conscientious eating decisions.

Additionally, these questions help people determine when they eat because of hunger and when they eat for other reasons.

WHY ARE YOU EATING?

Ask yourself these questions to get to the motivations behind emotional eating.

- What percentage of the time do you stop and ask, "Am I hungry?" when you have a craving or feel like eating?
- What does physical hunger feel like to you? Describe your symptoms of physical hunger.
- Do you ever eat when you are aware that you are not hungry?
- How do you decide what you are going to eat?
- How do you decide when to stop eating?

After working with Kevin for several weeks, his therapist recommended nutrition counseling. While Kevin was ready to let go of the food, he had become so disconnected from a normal eating routine he was having a difficult time getting back on track. Here is one of Kevin's early entries:

Kevin's Food Journal

ITEM	RESPONSE
Time of meal or snack.	A.M. *10* P.M.
Where was meal or snack consumed?	*In the living room*
Did you eat alone or with someone else?	*Alone.*
Were you aware of being physically hungry when you began eating?	*No.*
If not, were you aware of any other emotions, or thoughts, such as boredom, anger, loneliness, depression, etc.	*I just felt numb.*
How did you decide what to eat?	*I knew there was ice cream in the freezer and I couldn't get my mind off of it.*
How did you feel when you were finished eating? Were you full, not full, or overly full? Were you satisfied? Were you energized or did you experience a lack of energy after consuming this meal or snack?	*Overly full.* *Yes.* *I felt sluggish and sleepy.*
How did you decide when to stop eating?	*I don't know. I think it was when I got too uncomfortable.*
If you could re-do this meal to produce a better outcome, what would you have done differently if anything?	*Talked to Kelly or read.*

Kevin found the journals extremely useful for identifying his patterns. The evening was a high-risk time when most of his emotional eating occurred. This is a time of day when many people feel depressed and run into trouble. Through counseling and food therapy, Kevin eventually realized that the unstructured evening hours time allowed his stress and grief to surface. When he's not busy, Kevin is no longer distracted from his thoughts and feelings of grief and anxiety. "During the day I'm preoccupied with work," he said. "But once things quiet down, and I'm home,

I can feel the anxiety and pain start to take over. It feels like a ton of bricks sitting on my chest."

To avoid experiencing his emotions, he would reach for ice cream and cookies. Kevin was literally numbing or stuffing down his feelings with food. By eating and becoming uncomfortably full, Kevin was able to take the focus off the uncomfortable emotional feelings he didn't want to face. "The eating is almost like an out of body experience, like floating. I don't feel anything. It's like an escape," he explained. "After I've binged I'm just so sleepy and full that I want to shut down. If I don't eat, I'll think and think and think and I won't be able to fall asleep."

The journals helped Kevin make these connections. He became more and more aware of what he was doing in the moment he was doing it, rather than realizing what had happened after the fact. Awareness allows people to see choices. In food therapy, we use the analogy of the lights suddenly turning on to describe this epiphany. With the lights on, Kevin could see himself standing at a crossroads. He knew where he was and how he was feeling and he had to make a conscious decision about which path to take. At times, he chose to use food rather than experiencing his feelings or finding positive ways to address them. However, as time went on, comfort eating felt less satisfying to Kevin.

"Once I became more aware of what was going on, I'd kind of wake up as I bit into a cookie and think to myself, 'Kevin, what are you doing?' I knew the food was just a distraction, not a solution, and I realized it was time to get at the root of the problem." Kevin's therapy also helped him work through his grief and anxiety so they did not build up to a breaking point.

Stepping Away from Emotional Eating

YOU CAN'T STOP eating for emotional reasons in one day. It's a gradual process that requires achieving several important steps, outlined here:

Step One: Catch Yourself
Notice the minute you start thinking of food.

Step Two: Check In with Your Hunger Scale
Are you actually hungry?

Step Three: Check In With Your Emotions
If you're not hungry, are you emotional?

Step Four: Explore Your Emotions
Ask yourself, "What am I feeling?" Be as specific as possible. "I'm upset" or "I'm bored" is not descriptive enough. Are you sad? Angry? Scared? Most unpleasant feelings can be described in a variation of one of these fundamental emotions.

Step Five: Think About How to Address That Emotion
Ask yourself, "What can I do to express that feeling that does not involve eating or any negative side effects?" Activities that help you let out or express anger, for example, are very different from activities that release sadness. When I'm sad, I like to cuddle with my cats or brush their fur. They are soft and affectionate and feel soothing and comforting. But if I'm angry, I rarely go near the cats. I do something more active: clean and scrub the kitchen, do yard work, listen and sing to loud music, or exercise. Use trial and error to find nondestructive activities that allow you to address your feelings. It's important that the activity you choose gets to the root of the feeling and doesn't just repress it or detach you from it (as food can). If the activity doesn't allow you to connect with or release your feelings, it's only a distraction, just like food.

Emotional eaters use food to deal with emotions. When you're aware of the emotion or feeling that is surfacing, you cannot solve or fix the circumstances that are causing you to feel this way, but you can address the feelings in a healthier way.

What "works" for one person may not work for another. For example, one of my clients soothed himself with ice cream when he felt sad. He was skeptical that anything else could make him feel as good as Häagen-Dazs Butter Pecan ice cream. However, he was tired of experiencing the downside of using food was he was sad: weight gain, discomfort and blood sugar problems. When he started to look for a substitute activity, he discussed it with his wife. She recommended doing what she does—watching a sad movie and crying to let it out. Not surprisingly, while this did wonders for her, it didn't work for him. After trying several activities he found that painting or writing both allowed him to feel better so he didn't "need" food. While it didn't feel exactly like ice cream, it felt good enough to alleviate his sadness and didn't cause any negative side effects.

In time and with the help of his counselor and Kelly, Kevin's journal looked like this:

Kevin's Food Journal

ITEM	RESPONSE
Time of meal or snack.	A.M. 9 P.M.
Where was meal or snack consumed?	Snack
Did you eat alone or with someone else?	With Kelly
Were you aware of being physically hungry when you began eating?	Yes. We had a light dinner at 5:30. I could feel an emptiness in my stomach.
If not, were you aware of any other emotions, or thoughts, such as boredom, anger, loneliness, depression, etc.	
How did you decide what to eat?	Kelly and I talked about what we had and what sounded good. We made popcorn.
How did you feel when you were finished eating? Were you full, not full, or overly full? Were you satisfied? Were you energized or did you experience a lack of energy after consuming this meal or snack?	Full. Yes. Neutral.
How did you decide when to stop eating?	Surprisingly, I just got to a point where I didn't want any more.
If you could re-do this meal to produce a better outcome, what would you have done differently if anything?	Maybe had water instead of diet soda with the popcorn.

While it was not an overnight process, Kevin eventually used these tools to find ways to eat that weren't controlled by his emotions. As he worked through his feelings and food issues, he became more open and communicative with Kelly. When, what, and how much he ate shifted.

The real test will come when another life event jostles Kevin. His challenge will be to get through a crisis without turning to food to numb his feelings. But if he maintains his emotional awareness, talks to Kelly, and finds healthy coping mechanisms like talking to someone he trusts, he should be okay.

16

Your Diet Is Driving Me Crazy!

DEALING WITH OBSESSIVE DIETING

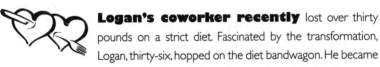 **Logan's coworker recently** lost over thirty pounds on a strict diet. Fascinated by the transformation, Logan, thirty-six, hopped on the diet bandwagon. He became fanatical about his intake. At first, Jesse, his thirty-five-year-old live-in boyfriend, thought the fanaticism wouldn't last. But as time went on, Logan became more and more militant. He refused to eat foods with sugar or carbohydrates, meticulously counted his daily fat grams, and gave Jesse a hard time about his diet. Grocery shopping, dining out, doing anything food-related together became a nightmare. In the food store, Jesse would lose it when Logan refused to go down the cookie or candy aisle. "I can't even look at it!" he'd say. Or they'd fight over whether or not to buy the ultra low carb beer that Jesse hates. "We have to get the low-carb—it's the only kind I can have," Logan would hiss. Sometimes Logan would chide Jesse about what he put in the cart, saying "I can't believe you want bananas. Do you know how much sugar are in those?!?" Logan is delighted with his weight loss, but Jesse is fed up. He blames Logan's mood swings, crankiness, and irritability on the diet. Lately they just aren't communicating at all.

Anyone who has been on a strict diet or been in a relationship with someone on a strict diet knows how food restriction wreaks havoc on emotions. Irritability, mood swings, and edginess are all side effects of strict dieting. But, in our weight-focused world, dieters are often willing to accept these consequences for the great weight loss reward. In fact, obsessive dieting is somewhat common. According to the American Dietetic Association, approximately 25 percent of men and 45 percent of women are on a diet on any given day.

Jesse and Logan were speaking different dietary languages. Jesse enjoys food, views it as nourishment, and a source of enjoyment. Logan, on the other hand, sees food as a way to control his weight. It's difficult for couples with such diverse food relationships to find common ground.

This food attitude questionnaire helps couples like Logan and Jesse find that happy medium:

What's Your Food Attitude?

QUESTION	RESPONSE
In general, describe the way you feel about food. Write down the first thing that comes to mind.	
Why do you eat the way you do?	
How do you think your feelings about food differ from your partner's?	
List the pros of eating the way you do.	
List the cons of eating the way you do.	

QUESTION	RESPONSE
Is there anything you would like to change about the way you currently eat?	
Realistically, how long do you think you will be able maintain your current way of eating?	
What bothers you about your partner's way of eating?	
How do your food-related differences affect your relationship?	

After each partner completes the worksheet, exchange papers and read each other's responses. Then answer the following:

WHAT DID YOU LEARN ABOUT EACH OTHER'S FOOD ATTITUDES?

◆ What surprised you about your partner's response?
◆ How are your answers similar? What food attitudes do you share?
◆ How can you support each other's goals?
◆ How are you willing to compromise?

This *honesty* activity is designed to give Jesse and Logan valuable insight into their own as well as each other's food mind-sets. Logan may realize that his strict diet is not a long-term solution for maintaining a healthy weight. If Jesse's views are presented in a thorough and neutral way, Logan may be able to see that the diet creates more negative than positive energy.

Here are Logan's responses:

QUESTION	RESPONSE
In general, describe the way you feel about food. Write down the first thing that comes to mind.	*Right now I fear food. I feel like I need to take control of my weight by eliminating a lot of food from my diet.*
Why do you eat the way you do?	*To lose weight—period.*
How do you think your feelings about food differ from your partner's?	*Oh, Jesse doesn't really have a problem with food. He doesn't get dieting at all.*
List the pros of eating the way you do.	*Control, rules, concrete guidelines. Sometimes it's just easier to limit myself than try to practice "moderation."*
List the cons of eating the way you do.	*It causes a lot of tension between us. Food has become one of the main issues we talk about now. Also, it's starting to wear on me. It's getting harder to stick with.*
Is there anything you would like to change about the way you currently eat?	*I wish I could eat whatever I want and still lose weight—who doesn't? I'd like to have more variety but I don't really know how.*
Realistically, how long do you think you will be able maintain your current way of eating?	*Yikes. Realistically, I know I can't do this forever. I get a high when I'm losing weight but I'm already thinking about cheating. Dieting isn't fun.*
What bothers you about your partner's way of eating?	*I wish I didn't obsess about food like Jesse. It doesn't bother me, but I'm envious.*
How do your food-related differences affect your relationship?	*We argue a lot more now.*

And, here are Jesse's answers:

QUESTION	RESPONSE
In general, describe the way you feel about food. Write down the first thing that comes to mind.	*I love it! I don't like being restricted. I don't think it's healthy to put foods in good and bad categories—I really do believe in "everything in moderation."*
Why do you eat the way you do?	*Because it feels good!*
How do you think your feelings about food differ from your partner's?	*Night and day.*
List the pros of eating the way you do.	*I don't spend too much time or energy thinking about what I eat. I enjoy food, eat what I want, stop when I'm full—that's it.*
List the cons of eating the way you do.	*I know it's hard for Logan. Food doesn't control me so I don't have to control it but I know Logan struggles with this.*
Is there anything you would like to change about the way you currently eat?	*No.*
Realistically, how long do you think you will be able maintain your current way of eating?	*Forever.*
What bothers you about your partner's way of eating?	*Ugh. He's so militant! He drives me crazy reading every label and flipping if he goes over by three grams of fat. It's really consuming him.*
How do your food-related differences affect your relationship?	*Going out to eat is a nightmare— there's hardly anyplace he can find something that meets his strict criteria—he usually gets a salad then complains about how bored and unsatisfied he feels. So much of our conversation revolves around his diet.*

By completing this *honesty* exercise and discussing what they learned from each other's food attitude, Jesse discovered how complicated Logan's relationship with food is. Until now, he didn't really know how difficult it was for Logan to deal with food. Now that he understands his motivations and his challenges, Jesse can help Logan reach his goals without hurting their relationship.

Even if Jesse and Logan agree to disagree about dieting, they have openly sorted through their feelings and achieved *honesty* by explaining their food attitudes. They've also generated ideas for the next *phase—compromise*.

To make compromise work, Logan and Jesse need to discuss their expectations. Too often, one partner feels let down because his or her expectations aren't met. Many times, this happens because of misunderstandings. Often a partner is confused by his or her partner's disappointment because their expectations were so different. It's easier to discover expectation by verbalizing them.

To that end, Logan and Jesse completed the following final exercise which you can work on as well:

GRADE YOUR RELATIONSHIP

Use a traditional academic grading scale to create a relationship report card.

A = stellar
B = above average
C = average
D = below average
F = failing miserably

Choose one problematic food-related scenario like going out to dinner, cooking together or grocery shopping. In the center column, each partner write outs his description of an "A" behavior, a "B" behavior, a "C" behavior, a "D" behavior, and an "F" behavior. An "A" behavior is stellar, the most you can hope for. An "F" is the worst, what would be the biggest disappointment to you. In the third column, mark an X next to the grade your partner earns.

For example, let's say a couple is having trouble with romance. The hurt partner might describe his or her expectations for Valentine's Day and then grade his or her partner's behavior.

Valentine's Day

GRADE	YOUR DESCRIPTION OF PASSING AND FAILING BEHAVIOR	HOW YOU GRADE YOUR PARTNER'S LATEST PERFORMANCE
A (or what your partner can do to pass with flying colors)	Surprise trip or well-planned picnic. Flowers. Lots of affection.	
B	Flowers, affection, and a homemade card.	
C	Store-bought card and a hug.	X
D	Saying Happy Valentines Day and giving me a hug.	
F	Not acknowledging Valentines Day at all.	

If one partner was failing to meet the other's expectations for Valentine's Day, he or she could learn exactly how from this report card. If your partner expects flowers, a surprise, and affection, and you're showing up with a card and a hug, you're falling short of expectations and causing disappointment—possibly without even realizing it. Without communicating expectations to each other, you may not understand how or why your partner is let down. If you discuss what each of you consider appropriate for Valentines Day, and agree on an A behavior, you'll get on the same page and be less likely to disappoint or expect too much from each other.

Logan and Jesse wrote down the best possible and worst possible behaviors for grocery shopping, an errand that often leads to arguments. Here is Logan's relationship report card:

My Partner's Grocery Shopping Behavior

GRADE	YOUR DESCRIPTION OF PASSING AND FAILING BEHAVIOR	PARTNER'S CURRENT GRADE
A	Helping me read labels to avoid foods that are not on my diet, not purchasing and bringing food into the house I can't have, supporting me fully—not trying to convince me to give up on my diet or argue with me.	
B	Fully supporting what I'm doing even if he wants to do his own thing.	
C	Trying to learn more about my diet.	
D	Not supporting but not helping me either.	
F	Constantly nagging me and arguing with me throughout the trip about my diet.	X

And, here's Jesse's report card:

My Partner's Grocery Shopping Behavior

GRADE	YOUR DESCRIPTION OF PASSING AND FAILING BEHAVIOR	PARTNER'S CURRENT GRADE
A	Realizing that this diet is way too restrictive and unrealistic and letting go for the sake of our relationship.	
B	Listening to my point of view and compromising on some aspects of the diet.	
C	Not expecting me to change my way of eating even if he wants to—basically, agreeing to disagree.	
D	Not listening to my point of view at all and expecting me to support it even though I don't agree and feel it's hurting us.	
F	Being militant about his diet, basically putting the diet before us.	X

The only thing Logan and Jesse have in common is that the other's behavior deserves an "F"! The challenge here is to come up with one grading scale they both agree on. If they can accomplish this, neither will feel let down.

Together, they came up with this scale for grocery shopping:

GRADE	YOUR DESCRIPTION OF PASSING AND FAILING BEHAVIOR	PARTNER'S CURRENT GRADE
A	Talking openly without getting emotional to try to understand the other's point of view then coming to a compromise.	
B	Taking the time to understand the other's point of view.	
C	Agreeing to disagree and allow the other to do his thing without arguing.	
D	Arguing about food.	
F	Arguing to the point of hurting each other/the relationship.	

In any tense situation, Logan and Jesse can continue to apply the grading scale, telling each other when something the other does is a definite "A" or an "F." Sometimes, in the heat of the moment, it's easier to tell someone that his or her comment is a "C" then it is to articulate how hurtful and upsetting it is.

A few weeks after our meeting, Jesse called to report that the exercises had a tremendous impact on his communication with Logan. He said, "I know keeping the weight off is important to Logan, he feels really good about himself when he's thin. But I want him to be healthy, so I bought him a cookbook that has all the nutrition facts. He was thrilled! He said, 'Jesse, this is an 'A.'"

With a new set of tools to keep the lines of communication open, Logan and Jesse are flourishing. They are finally able to really listen to each other. Logan has relaxed a little and adopted a more moderate way of eating that Jesse is more than willing to support.

17

Why Aren't You Having Anything?

UNDERSTANDING EATING DISORDERS

 **A year before they** were married, Penny, twenty-five, told Ian, twenty-seven, that she's struggled with a serious eating disorder since college. He knew she had been admitted to a few treatment facilities in the past, and still sees a therapist regularly, but he hoped she would recover. At times, she seemed fine, then inevitably something—a visit from her family, their move to a new neighborhood, and recent talk about starting a family—would trigger a setback. Lately, she'd become withdrawn again and lost weight. Most days, the only things she'd eat was a salad, a can of tuna, and gallons of diet Coke™. If they went out to eat, she would excuse herself from the table after eating, spend ten minutes in the ladies' room and come back to the table with watery eyes and a breath mint in her mouth. Although he tried, Ian couldn't understand Penny's struggle with anorexia and bulimia.

When Penny wasn't doing well, she didn't want to socialize, never laughed, and always rejected his sexual advances. He accepted it, and knew it was a source of pain for her, but he was frustrated at its impact on their lives. Ian knew Penny was diligently working with her therapist but he couldn't just sit on the sidelines and watch this play out. After two years he needed support himself and began searching the Internet. He came across my name in an article about eating disorders and contacted me. He said that up until this point, he trusted that things would get better and tried to be patient. Now he wants to understand what Penny is going through and find out how he can help.

Ian's confusion and frustration is understandable. I've worked with clients with moderate to severe eating disorders for over ten years, and the condition is emotional for everyone involved. From the outside, eating disorders appear irrational. It's difficult for anyone, especially a loved one, to understand why his or her partner can't just let go of the food and weight obsession that is literally killing them.

"Have you had any contact with Penny's therapist?" I asked.

"Well, I know Penny sees Dr. Allen for counseling but it's not like I've met her," he answered.

I asked if Penny was seeing a dietitian on a regular basis. He didn't think so.

"What about you?" I asked, "Do you have a support network to help you deal with your feelings about this?"

He said no. His family did not know about Penny's eating disorder. She was afraid they would think differently of her and Ian did not want to break Penny's trust by telling them. "And I wouldn't describe Penny's family as close or supportive," he added.

I shared the ground rules about helping someone with an eating disorder.

THE DO'S AND DON'TS OF HELPING A LOVED ONE WITH AN EATING DISORDER

Do

◆ Learn about eating disorders and become more familiar with what they are really about.

- Be there for support without being judgmental or critical.
- Be aware of your loved one's behavior by observing but not policing them.
- Ask your loved one what help he or she expects and needs from you.
- Realize that your loved one may not be completely honest with you about his or her behavior or recovery progression. Shame and secrecy are part of the disease.
- Request permission to communicate with the therapists or treatment team. They can help you understand where your loved one is in recovery, what goals they are currently working on, and how you can help.
- Realize that you cannot make your loved one get better. You are not responsible for another person's recovery.
- Focus on your loved ones feelings rather than his or her weight and eating behavior.
- Be patient. Recovery is not an overnight process.
- Get support for yourself and develop healthy coping mechanisms, like talking to someone you trust or finding ways to blow off steam.

Don't

- Focus on food or weight. These are symptoms and focusing on them can interfere with your loved one's ability to get to the root of the disorder.
- Enable your loved one by treating him or her like a child or allowing the person to avoid treatment.
- Discount the severity of the disorder by saying things like, "Why can't you just eat?" or "You look fine the way you are."
- Try to be your loved one's therapist, physician, or dietitian. Allow the trained professionals to provide this care.
- Talk about your own weight or food concerns around your loved one. That may trigger the person to restrict, binge, or purge even more.

- Assume that men don't have eating disorders.
- Believe that an eating disorder can be cured by sheer willpower.
- Threaten, lecture, or blame your loved one.
- Blame yourself. When it comes to an eating disorder, there is no one cause.

Why It's Important to Get Informed

EATING DISORDERS ARE an up and down battle. Your loved one will experience good days and bad days, and his or her behavior may often change. Those with eating disorders tend to be very secretive, and may be very good at hiding behaviors or making you think they are doing better than they are. By getting informed, you may learn that some of their "quirks" are really symptoms. For example, they may say they don't like bread or don't have a sweet tooth but these may actually just be excuses for not eating those foods. Learning more can help you not be fooled by the disease. Knowledge about the disease will help you understand the progression of recovery—what to expect, what not to expect, what to say, and what not to say. People who suffer from eating disorders are sensitive to the comments and actions of the people around them. By taking advantage of resources and reading up, you'll learn the most important things of all: how to *not* make it worse. These Web sites help outsiders understand eating disorders and the recovery process: www.something-fishy.org (This informative hub includes general information for significant others and support forums for sufferers as well as loved ones.); www.nationaleatingdisorders.org (The official site of the National Eating Disorders Association features treatment referrals, information on advocacy and the latest research news.); www.bulimia.com (A virtual bookstore for publications on anorexia, bulimia, binge eating, body image, and obesity.).

It's best if Ian is honest with Penny and tells her about our conversation and his Internet search. "Talk to her about wanting to learn more and help, but," I cautioned, "approach her very gently and lovingly. It's common for those struggling with recovery to become defensive or anxious when confronted about the disorder."

As with those who suffer from other diseases, like alcoholism, a person with an eating disorder can only get better when they are ready. It's difficult for Ian to watch Penny go through this and feel helpless. But he cannot make her better no matter how much he loves her.

I suggested Ian ask Penny to contact me if her therapist feels she could use the support of a dietitian. A few months later, she called. She thanked me for talking to her husband. "I know it's hard for him, and I'm glad he found someone who really understands," she said.

Her therapist suggested working with a dietitian again. Penny signed a release form that allowed me to communicate with her therapist, Dr. Allen. The doctor explained that Penny recently relapsed from her stable eating regime. She slipped back into her usual pattern of alternating between days of restrictive eating and overexercise followed by binging, vomiting, and using laxatives or diet pills.

Penny had been through nutrition counseling before, so when we met, I tried to reinforce what she had previously learned. We discussed her body's need for adequate nutrition and tools she can use to feel safer about following through with her balanced meal plan.

Penny listed all of the physical side effects she experienced when she was active in her eating disorder. The list included extreme fatigue, irritability and mood swings, getting sick frequently, missing her period, trouble sleeping, hair loss, and digestive problems.

Penny wrote these down on an index card. On the other side, she wrote the reasons her body needs food: to support and repair her vital organs, to support and repair muscles, and to support activity. When Penny was tempted to restrict, she could read the index cards to strengthen the rational voice within her. At the same time, the cards would help suppress the voice of the disorder that tells her things will be better if she controls her food and weight.

SIDE EFFECTS OF MY EATING DISORDER

- ◆ Fatigue
- ◆ Irritability and mood swings
- ◆ Frequent illness
- ◆ Missed periods
- ◆ Trouble sleeping
- ◆ Hair loss
- ◆ Digestive problems

WHY MY BODY NEEDS FOOD

- ◆ To support and repair vital organs
- ◆ To support and repair muscles
- ◆ To support activity and energy

Like most people with eating disorders, Penny knew her problem was hurting her husband. "I've been in treatment centers with women who had to leave their families to fully focus on recovery," she said. "And I don't want that to happen to me."

She wanted his support but she did not want to burden him. She knew he wouldn't bring it up because he was trying to respect her feelings. Dr. Allen was helping her get to a place where she could ask for and accept his help.

We worked to stabilize her eating and to help her feel comfortable nourishing her body. At the same time, she worked with Dr. Allen to find healthy ways to deal with the emotional issues projected onto her weight, body image, and food intake. After Dr. Allen scheduled several consultations with both her and Ian, she suggested the two of them come to see me together. Penny was finally ready to let Ian help.

"I don't want Ian to be the food police, looking over my shoulder at everything I eat to keep track of my food intake," she explained. "He never does that and that's one reason why we're married. My mother did that and it made me want to restrict or binge even more. I felt like I was under a microscope and couldn't be trusted. It was punitive. Ian has always given me my space but maybe I've let him give me too much space. I need to allow him to help."

"What would be the right balance?" I asked.

"Well, I need to talk about it without feeling judged. Dr. Allen helped me understand that because Ian fully accepts my eating disorder, in a way, he's stopping me from getting better," she said. "I need some accountability but not policing."

Role-playing is a great way to communicate difficult ideas like what Penny wants from Ian. I asked Penny to pretend to be Ian. Then I spoke, as Penny, and set the stage.

CYNTHIA AS PENNY
We are at home and you notice that while I made chicken pasta and salad for you I'm only eating salad. What are you going to do?

PENNY AS IAN
(She pauses, looks at Ian, then at me.)
Honey, why are you just eating salad?

CYNTHIA AS PENNY
I'm not very hungry.

PENNY AS IAN
Is everything okay? Are you upset about anything?

Penny started to cry and Ian put his arm around her. "That's what I need," she said, finally asking for his support. "With my parents it was always about the food or my weight. They'd say, You need to finish that. I just wanted them to ask me how I was feeling, what was wrong, what was going on with me, what was really going on."

Eating disorders aren't really about food but because they manifest that way, food becomes the focus. Penny may need some helpful reminders from Ian about why she needs to eat. However, the way he confronts her should be about *her,* not the food, or how her clothes are fitting.

He nodded and they both agreed to another role-play. This time they were themselves.

> ### CYNTHIA
> *You're out to dinner. After eating a meal and splitting a dessert Penny becomes distracted and says she's going to the ladies' room. What do you do, Ian?*

> ### IAN
> *(He hesitates, looks Penny in the eyes, and puts his hand on hers.)*
> *Are you sure you're okay?*

> ### PENNY
> *(She holds back tears.)*
> *I'm scared.*

> ### IAN
> *Why?*

> ### PENNY
> *I don't know.*

IAN

It's okay. Talk to me.

PENNY

(Tears stream down her face, and she clenches his hand.)

Penny can benefit from thinking more about the "high risk" situations like the holidays, parties, or restaurant meals when she might need more help from Ian. She'll do well to let him know that these are difficult times and ask for his support before, during, and after each occasion. Some find it useful to write up the list, give it to their partner, and mention the specific event a few days before it occurs.

PENNY'S LIST

Penny must remember that when Ian responds to her behavior, his goal is to work with her to overcome her disorder. His goal is not to judge her.

- ◆ List high-risk situations for Ian.
- ◆ Explain to him why these are difficult times and ask for his support before, during, and after each high-risk event.

IAN'S LIST

Ian needs to find supportive outlets. "Always remember that you are not responsible for Penny's recovery," I said. "You are there to help, not fix."

- ◆ Find supportive outlets, like website support groups (see page 186).

◆ Confide in a friend.

◆ Each week, ask Penny about her new goals.

ROLE-PLAYS AND RESPONSES

Using each other's lists, they can develop more role-plays to work on at home. After each scene, Penny can give Ian feedback about how his response made her feel as well as how it differs from what she needs.

◆ Act out additional role-plays at home based on Penny's list.

◆ Discuss how Ian's responses make Penny feel.

Penny still comes in on a regular basis. Ian's support has made a tremendous difference on her recovery. They are not quite ready to have a baby but Penny is much further into recovery than she was a year ago. Eating disorders involve step-by-step progress and require the ongoing help of a team of professionals and loved ones. The support of a partner can have a remarkable impact on long-term recovery.

Help with Eating Disorders

IF YOU OR a loved one is struggling with a serious eating disorder, seek outside help from a mental health professional who specializes in eating disorders. For more information, visit:

The National Association of Anorexia Nervosa and Associated Disorders: www.altrue.net/site/anadweb/

Acknowledgments

We would like to both acknowledge:

Thanks to Matthew Lore, for intelligent guidance, keen instincts, and comic relief. And most especially, thank you for understanding this book.

Thanks to Carole Bidnick for her infectious enthusiasm, tremendous professionalism and perpetual encouragement.

Francesca Castagnoli, Jim Oseland, and Nate Penn helped us shape our idea into words, and we appreciate every single piece of advice.

Thanks to Lori Ferme and Nicci Micco, who got this right away and brought the two of us together.

Caroline Pincus, thank you for your expert direction.

Two big thank-yous to Jack Bremen for his insights, thoughts, and technical support and to Michael Dolan for his careful attention and patience.

We thank Barbara Leone, Ann Dolan, EdM, Pio Andreotti, PsyD, Suzanne Wickham Beaird, Tammy Richards LeSure, and Dawn Jackson, RD for their thorough and thoughtful professional feedback.

And finally, we thank the wonderful staff at Marlowe & Company, especially Peter Jacoby for all his help and efficiency, Shona McCarthy, Wendie Carr, and Karen Auerbach.

Cynthia Sass acknowledges:

Thanks to my parents, Jim and Carol Crowell, my siblings, and every member of my Crowell, Sass, DeTota, and Salvagno families. And special thanks to Lynn, Steve, Rachael, Anna and Steven Miller, Kathy and Ron DeTota, and Steve DeTota, for their extraordinary gestures of love and support.

Thanks to the amazing group of women I am honored to call my friends, especially Beverly Hill, Amy Gerardo, Tonya Quillen, Stefanie Barry, and Sharon Hickman.

To the entire Public Relations Department of the American Dietetic Association: Thank you for granting me the honor of representing our association. I acknowledge Dr. Gail Frank, my ADA mentor, and to all of the ADA spokespeople for your tireless work on behalf of our profession.

I acknowledge my faculty and mentors at Syracuse University and the University of South Florida, especially Sarah Short, PhD, EdD, RD, Lois Schroeder, PhD, RD, Debbie Connolly, MA, RD, Jean Bowering, PhD, RD, and Kelli McCormack Brown PhD, CHES.

Thanks to all of my students who have taught me so much and helped me become a better teacher and practitioner.

I'd like express my gratitude to all of my clients for putting your trust in me, and making me feel like I have the best job in the world.

Finally, thanks to my coauthor, Denise Maher for her outstanding professionalism, talent, generosity, teamwork, and humor.

Denise Maher acknowledges:

This book would not have been possible without the support and cooperation of the following:

Carlene Bauer, Renata Bokalo, Angela Dolan, Meg D'Incecco, Brekke Fletcher, Cathy Garrard, Sheri Goldhirsch & Young Playwrights Inc., Tula Karras, Jeannine Magno, Trina Realmuto, Pat Singer, and Jane Webb.

Thanks to my family, especially James and Rita Maher, for always encouraging me and my writing.

Many thanks to everyone who shared their relationship food conflicts, ideas and insights: Sam Barclay, Anna Crafton, Clarissa Febles, MD, Amanda Gardner, Brook Gesser, Lori Goldberg, Bill Kuhne, Sara Lippmann, Roman Luba, Kevin Maher, Margery Miller, Amy Morelli, Kristen Muller, Hema Nair, Barry Neville, Rebecca Paller, Rebecca Rogers, Pia Rosen, Meredith Seeder, Jessica Shevitz, and Melissa Verril.

And thanks to my better half in book writing, Cynthia Sass, whose expertise, hard work and genuine drive to help people made the creative process a rewarding and gratifying endeavor.

Index